COUNSELLING SKILLS FOR
HEALTH PROFESSIONALS

FORTHCOMING TITLES

Research Methods for Therapists
Avril Drummond

Group Work in Occupational Therapy
Linda Finlay

Stroke: Recovery and Rehabilitation
Polly Laidler

Caring for the Neurologically Damaged Adult
Ruth Nieuwenhuis

HIV and Aids Care
S. Singh and L. Cusack

Speech and Language Disorders in Children
Dilys A. Treharne

Spinal Cord Rehabilitation
Karen Whalley-Hammell

THERAPY IN PRACTICE SERIES

Edited by Jo Campling

This series of books is aimed at 'therapists' concerned with rehabilitation in a very broad sense. The intended audience particularly includes occupational therapists, physiotherapists and speech therapists, but many titles will also be of interest to nurses, physchologists, medical staff, social workers, teachers or volunteer workers. Some volumes are interdisciplinary, others are aimed at one particular profession. All titles will be comprehensive but concise, and practical but with due reference to relevant theory and evidence. They are not research monographs but focus on professional practice, and will be of value to both students and qualified personnel.

1. Occupation Therapy for Children with Disabilities
   Dorothy E. Penso
2. Living Skills for Mentally Handicapped People
   Christine Peck and Chia Swee Hong
3. Rehabilitation of the Older Patient
   Edited by Amanda J. Squires
4. Physiotherapy and the Elderly Patient
   Paul Wagstaff and Davis Coakley
5. Rehabilitation of the Severely Brain-Injured Adult
   Edited by Ian Fussey and Gordon Muir Giles
6. Communication Problems in Elderly People
   Rosemary Gravell
7. Occupational Therapy Practice in Psychiatry
   Linda Finlay
8. Working with Bilingual Language Disability
   Edited by Deirdre M. Duncan
9. Counselling Skills for Health Professional
   Philip Burnard
10. Teaching Interpersonal Skills
    A handbook of experiential learning for health professionals
    Philip Burnard
11. Occupational Therapy for Stroke Rehabilitation
    Simon B. N. Thompson and Maryanne Morgan
12. Assessing Physically Disabled People at Home
    Kathy Maczka
13. Acute Head Injury
    Practical management in rehabilitation
    Ruth Garner
14. Practical Physiotherapy with Older People
    Lucinda Smyth et al.
15. Keyboard, Graphic and Handwriting Skills
    Helping people with motor disabilities
    Dorothy E. Penso
16. Community Occupational Therapy with Mentally Handicapped Adults
    Debbie Isaac
17. Autism
    Professional perspectives and practice
    Edited by Kathryn Ellis

18. Multiple Sclerosis
Approaches to management
Edited by Lorraine De Souza

19. Occupational Therapy in Rheumatology
An holistic approach
Lynne Sandles

20. Breakdown of Speech
Causes and remediation
Nancy R. Milloy

21. Coping with Stress in the Health Professions
A practical guide
Philip Burnard

22. Speech, Communication Problems in Psychiatry
Rosemary Gravell and Jenny France

23. Limb Amputation
From aetiology to rehabilitation
Rosalind Ham and Leonard Cotton

24. Management in Occupational Therapy
Zielfa B. Maslin

25. Rehabilitation in Parkinson's Disease
Edited by Francis I. Caird

26. Exercise Physiology for Health Professionals
Stephen R. Bird

27. Therapy for the Burn Patient
Annette Leveridge

28. Effective Communication Skills for Health Professionals
Philip Burnard

29. Ageing, Healthy and in Control
An alternative approach to maintaining the health of older people
Steve Scrutton

30. The Early Identification of Language Impairment in Children
Edited by James Law

31. An Introduction to Communication Disorders
Diana Syder

32. Writing for Health Professionals
A manual for writers
Philip Burnard

33. Brain Injury Rehabilitation
A neuro-functional approach
Jo Clark-Wilson and Gordon Muir Giles

34. Living with Continuing Perceptuo-motor Difficulties
Theory and strategies to help children, adolescents and adults
Dorothy E. Penso

35. Psychology and Counselling for Health Professionals
Edited by Rowan Bayne and Paula Nicholson

36. Occupational Therapy for Orthopaedic Conditions
Dina Penrose

37. Teaching Students in Clinical Settings
Jackie Stengelhofen

Counselling Skills for Health Professionals

PHILIP BURNARD

University of Wales College of Medicine

CHAPMAN & HALL
London · Glasgow · New York · Tokyo · Melbourne · Madras

Published by Chapman & Hall, 2–6 Boundary Row, London SE1 8HN

Chapman & Hall, 2–6 Boundary Row, London SE1 8HN, UK

Chapman & Hall, 29 West 35th Street, New York NY10001, USA

Chapman & Hall Japan, Thomson Publishing Japan, Hirakawacho Nemoto Building, 7F, 1-7-11 Hirakawa-cho, Chiyoda-ku, Tokyo 102, Japan

Chapman & Hall Australia, Thomas Nelson Australia, 102 Dodds Street, South Melbourne, Victoria 3205, Australia

Chapman & Hall India, R. Seshadri, 32 Second Main Road, CIT East, Madras 600 035, India

First edition 1989
Reprinted 1990, 1991, 1992 (twice)

© 1989 Philip Burnard

Typeset in 10/12 Times by Mayhew Typesetting, Bristol
Printed in Great Britain by St Edmundsbury Press Ltd,
Bury St Edmunds, Suffolk

ISBN 0 412 32000 2

Contents

Acknowledgements   ix

Introduction   xi

1. What is counselling?   1

2. Psychological approaches to counselling   23

3. Counselling and self-awareness   39

4. Basic principles and considerations   66

5. Maps of the counselling relationship   87

6. Counselling skills I: listening and attending   102

7. Counselling skills II: client-centred skills   115

8. Counselling skills III: helping with feelings   127

9. Problems and support in counselling   139

10. Learning counselling skills   152

11. Counselling-skills exercises   163

References   184

Further reading   189

Index   197

For Sally, Aaron and Rebecca

Acknowledgements

Thanks go to many people – friends, clients, students and teachers – past and present who have taught me about counselling and ways of teaching it. Particular thanks to my friend and colleague, Paul Morrison, who has frequently made me think and rethink during the course of writing this book. Thanks are also offered to Jane Millar, Sarah Jowett, Joe Beighton and Kay Smithers for their help in offering me background information on physiotherapy, district nursing, social work and health visiting.

Thanks to Jo Campling and to Tim Hardwick of Chapman and Hall for their help during the writing and editing. Finally, special thanks to my wife, Sally and to my children Aaron and Rebecca for their help, patience and support. They have made all the difference.

Introduction

Counselling is a practical activity. The aim of this book is to offer
a practical framework to enable those who work in the health professions to develop a range of counselling skills. It will also offer a
theoretical grounding that may serve to inform counselling practice.

The book is aimed at any of those people who work in the health
professions: nurses, medical staff, occupational therapists,
physiotherapists, speech therapists, social workers, teachers of
various sorts and voluntary workers. It does not seek to provide
information specific to the work of those groups but aims at demysti-
fying counselling and making the skills involved available to them
all. The book assumes that the professional working in a particular
group will already have their own body of knowledge regarding their
work. This book will supplement that knowledge and extend the
range of caring skills. Throughout the book, practical examples of
the principles under discussion are offered. These help to make the
abstract concrete. They also serve to apply the skills described to a
variety of health-care settings.

A problem arises over gender and trying to avoid sexist language.
I have been unable to find a solution to it and have referred to the
counsellor as she and the client as he. No sexism is intended but the
usage may have made for clarity and ease of reading. Throughout
the text, the term counsellor is used to refer to the health professional working in that capacity. The term client is used to denote the
person receiving help. It is acknowledged that some will prefer the
terms patient, resident or person. Again, it is hoped that the usage
adopted makes for clarity and ease of reading.

The first part of the book explores various theoretical issues: what
counselling is, approaches to counselling practice, the issue of self-
awareness in counselling and maps of the counselling process. The
second part considers specific counselling skills: listening and attending, client-centred counselling interventions, coping with feelings,
problems and support for the counsellor. The last part of the book
focuses on practical methods of developing counselling skills and is
addressed to three groups: the person working on her own, those
working in pairs and those learning counselling in small groups.
Practical suggestions are offered for the setting up and running of
such groups. The book then offers a range of counselling-skills exercises that may be used by any of the aforementioned three groups

of people. The emphasis, throughout, is on making the skills of counselling clear and manageable without glossing over human complexities and the theoretical aspects of the task. The book closes with a bibliography containing references, recommended and further reading.

It is hoped that with the increasing call for health education and for self-direction in health care, the skills explored in this book will be useful to a wide range of people: from the individual who wishes to explore the field for the first time, to the tutor who wants practical ideas about running counselling-skills workshops. We all have problems in our lives and counselling offers one means of exploring and relieving them. I do not believe that counselling is something that should and can only be done by trained professionals. I do not believe, either, that there is any one right way to go about counselling. We must avoid becoming too clever about the degree to which we believe that what we do affects other people. In the end, it is the person referred to as the client who makes a difference to his own life. In the end, it is the client who sorts himself out. George Kelly, the personal-construct psychologist offers a very practical point of view when he says that:

The only valid way to live one's life is to get on with it.
(Kelly, 1969)

I know, however, that with practice we can all learn to listen more carefully to other people and resist the temptation to rush in and try to 'fix things' for them. Listening remains the basis of all effective counselling. This book is aimed at developing that skill and building on it. I welcome any comments or suggestions you may have about the book.

Philip Burnard
Caerphilly
South Wales

Spring 1988

1

What is counselling?

We are all counsellors. Anyone who works in one of the health professions and comes into contact with people who are distressed in any way, whether psychologically, physically, spiritually or practically, offers counselling help. In this sense, counselling is something that is familiar to everyone. There need be no mystique about it. Nor should it be something that is reserved for a particular group of professionals who call themselves counsellors. Thus the discussion is already focused on familiar territory. Like all such familiar territory, however, we can always get to know it better. The aim of this book is to explore some of the many faces of counselling and to encourage the health professional to identify ways in which her counselling skills may be improved. All skills, after all, are learned. This is true irrespective of any particular psychological point of view we may hold. Whether or not we would tend to call ourselves behaviourally, psychodynamically or humanistically oriented, there seems little doubt that we learn and develop skills as we grow, train and live. It would seem difficult to argue otherwise and to say that we may be born with counselling skills!

If it is true that we learn skills in this way, then it would also appear to be true that we can improve our interpersonal skills. This book focuses on that argument and is a practical guide to enable the already functioning counsellor to become a better one. The practical skills described in this volume may be used in a wide variety of situations from talking through a period of work-related stress with a friend to coping with a client in emotional crisis. The skills involved in these situations turn out to be remarkably similar. There are basic human skills that can be applied in almost all human situations. There are also pitfalls that may be avoided. These are also discussed.

Human problems are rarely profession specific. Whilst, clearly, the doctor deals with aspects of the human situation in a different sort of way than would the physiotherapist, and the nurse is responsible for different aspects of care to the speech therapist, in the end, the difficulties that arise through the process of living turn out to be the domain of all health professionals. In a way, we all suffer the same sorts of problems, or as Carl Rogers, the late founder of client-centred counselling noted: 'what is most personal is most universal' (Rogers, 1967). The fact that we live at all, gives us a clue to the sorts of problems that anyone can suffer. The fact that we live at all also gives us the clue to how others may overcome their problems. This is not to say that everyone perceives their problems in the same sort of way, but to note that suffering is universal. Anyone who is concerned for another person's health needs, necessarily, to be concerned for what may be called that person's problems in living. It is towards these problems in living that counselling is directed.

The **process** of counselling may be defined as the means by which one person helps another to clarify their life situation and to decide upon further lines of action. Lack of clarity often brings anxiety. We are frightened by what we do not know or understand. Such fear and lack of clarity often leads, in turn, to inaction. This is often true in the health-care setting. The patient who is suffering from chronic illness often finds it difficult to plan ahead, often through fear born out of lack of information about his condition. The aim of counselling must be to free the person being counselled to live more fully and such fuller living comes through **action**. In the end, then, counselling must have a practical aim. It can never be 'only talk' to a theoretical or academic end. It must seek to enable the client to become confident enough to choose a particular course of action and see it through. In this sense, counselling is also a process of befriending, of supporting the other person. Again, such befriending is familiar to all of us and is a vital part of any person's job in the health professions. The nurse befriends the psychiatric patient when in the role of community psychiatric nurse. The social worker very clearly befriends the families with whom she works and the general practitioner becomes a friend to his patients. This concept of befriending will be useful when it comes to discussing the qualities of an effective counsellor in Chapter 3.

COUNSELLING AND THE HEALTH PROFESSIONAL

Counselling, then, involves listening, helping and befriending. In these respects, it is the central feature of the work of all health professionals in whatever branch. Examples of the application of counselling skills and principles are numerous and a few examples of such applications are identified below. The examples of health professions and applications are not claimed to be exhaustive of either.

1. *Medicine:*
   (a) helping clients who experience emotional, social and relationship problems
   (b) facing family crises and difficulties
   (c) clarifying diagnoses

2. *Nursing:*
   (a) coping with dying and bereaved people
   (b) assisting relatives and colleagues
   (c) handling other people's emotional release

3. *Occupational therapy:*
   (a) talking through personal issues with clients individually and in groups
   (b) discussing coping skills
   (c) enabling clients to regain their ability to live independently

4. *Physiotherapy:*
   (a) helping clients to adapt to long-term disability
   (b) helping people to regain motivation in the rehabilitation process

5. *Teaching:*
   (a) talking through academic problems
   (b) vocational guidance
   (c) pastoral work

6. *Voluntary work:*
   (a) listening to clients' problems in living
   (b) supporting other health professionals

7. *Social work:*
   (a) enabling the client and family group to clarify problems and identify goals
   (b) enabling client advocacy

3

8. *Speech therapy:*
   (a) discussing problems with clients
   (b) talking to parents and other relatives

Clearly, many of these aspects of the health professionals' role overlap with each other and interrelate between professional roles. It is, however, also clear that counselling forms an integral part of the daily work of all health professionals. The skills described and discussed in this book will enable all such professionals to enhance their daily practice, whatever their particular focus. Thus the skills may be used by nurses working with the elderly and the mentally ill as well as by those working in rehabilitation and general medicine. Physiotherapists will find the sections on listening, client-centred counselling and on coping with emotion useful when helping both the acutely and chronically ill. Occupational therapists may well find that what are described as counselling skills in this book are skills that can be used daily when working with both the individual and the group in psychiatric and in general practice.

VARIETIES OF COUNSELLING

In order to identify the variety of aspects of the counselling process, it may be useful to identify different sorts of counselling. Counselling is not one set of skills to be used in a narrow range of situations but a differing and often idiosyncratic mixture of personal qualities, practical skills and interpersonal verbal and nonverbal behaviours that combine to make up a particularly caring aspect of the health professional's job. Later, too, it will be necessary to consider how the counsellor needs to take care of herself, as human caring of the sort being described here, takes its toll. We cannot be involved with others without that contact touching our own lives, our belief and value systems and our emotional make-up. As carers, we need to take care of ourselves.

Supportive counselling

Perhaps the most frequently called-for type of counselling is that in which we are asked to support the client. This may take the form of acting as a sounding board for their ideas, plans or suggestions. The primary skill required in acting in such a fashion is the skill of listening. To truly listen to another person is perhaps the most caring action of all. Listening is more fully discussed in Chapter 6 of this book. In that chapter various aspects of the listening process are explored and the reader is offered practical suggestions on how to improve their listening skills. In no sense is this a question of 'teaching your grandmother to suck eggs!' Whilst we all have experience of listening, so do we all have experience of only half listening, of being caught up in our own concerns, of rehearsing our answers! All of these activities distract us from the process of offering true support to the other person. If we are to offer supportive counselling, we must learn to give ourselves almost completely to the other person for the period that we are with them.

Supportive counselling also calls for more than the ability to listen. It calls for the capacity to imagine how the world seems to be viewed by the client, to offer what Rogers' calls 'empathic understanding' (Rogers, 1967; 1983). The degree to which it is possible to offer such empathy is open to question and this, too, is taken up in a later chapter.

Another important aspect of any discussion of offering support on a professional basis is the question of commitment to the process. Alistair Campbell discusses this issue eloquently in his book *Paid to Care* (Campbell, 1984). There seems to be something very slightly curious about the fact that any of us involved in caring for others in a way that involves deep understanding is also doing it as a job! Perhaps in setting out as a counsellor, we need to consider our motives for undertaking such a task at all. Whilst altruism or true caring for the needs of others must be at work in the counselling process, it must be reasonable to assume that in supporting others, we are also getting something out of the process for ourselves!

Supportive counselling occurs in a variety of settings. The physiotherapist who sees a client through the lengthy rehabilitation process that often occurs following road accidents, in encouraging that person, is also offering a type of supportive counselling. It is she who often has to listen to the client's darker thoughts and feelings, during the inevitable troughs in the process of rehabilitation. The voluntary worker in a general hospital often undertakes supportive counselling as a very specific part of her role. Very often, she has the time that other health carers do not have (or do not claim to have!). General practitioners, in allowing their patients to verbalize their family problems and to talk through anxieties are also offering such counselling. Student nurses, working in a wide range of settings, from working with the mentally handicapped to caring for the terminally ill, regularly face situations in which they are asked to be supportive.

All health professionals have to help patients and clients adapt to various situations, from learning to live with paralysis to coping with a colostomy. In many of these situations, patients and clients have to adjust to a different body image, a changed perception of self. Fortunately, such adaptation can be made but the health professional who is able to offer adequate and appropriate support can do much to smooth the process.

The skills outlined in this book can enable health professionals to survive the pressure of such situations. For too long, nurses and other caring professionals have been expected to cope with the process of bearing other people's problems. Such a process can be emotionally exhausting, particularly if the carers concerned have been given no training in offering such support. In the past, the 'grin and bear it' school tended to encourage caring professionals to either cope in such situations or to feel guilty if they did not. As we have seen, counselling skills are learned through one means or another. It would seem sensible that they are also taught as part of all health professionals' training!

Informative counselling

Health professionals, by nature of the education and training, develop a considerable amount of knowledge about the domain in which they work. Much of this knowledge relates directly to how people work. Clearly, different sorts of medical practitioners have different sorts of very specific knowledge about physiology, disease and health. Occupational therapists, on the other hand, have knowledge about how people may restore their health through activity and relearning. So far, so good. Clients often ask for very specific information about the nature of their health or illness and such information is what makes up the notion of informative counselling. Clearly, the client requires accurate and understandable information and information on which he can act. A current example of how people may require informative counselling is the spread of the AIDS virus. People increasingly require an understanding of how they should conduct their sexual relationships or manage the administration of intravenous drugs. Workers within the health professions may also seek informative counselling from other health professionals in order that (a) they may use the information to care for others and (b) they may use the information in their own lives.

All this is fairly unproblematic, or so it would seem. People require information. Someone else has that information. All that is left is for the information to be handed over! In reality, of course, it is rarely that simple. Any information concerning my body or my life concerns me, not in a detached, academic way but in a very personal sense. Thus, the giving of informative counselling in the health professions is unlike the giving of information in, say, the estate-agency business. In the latter, we are dealing (at least to some degree) with impersonal facts. In the former situation, the case is overladen with an emotional aspect that calls for sympathy, empathy, tact and considerable skill. To give another person information about themselves or about relatives or friends is an emotional process. Whilst the information must be accurate, the delivery of that information must be appropriate to the needs of the receiver.

Another problem arises here. The giving of information about illness, health or physiology seems to be reasonably unproblematic if we can develop the skill of giving it sensitively. In the domain of problems in living alluded to previously (p. 2), however, the situation is very different. When it comes to giving another person information about how to live their lives, we are on much less certain ground. Many would argue, perhaps, that the only person who is truly able to furnish information about a person's problems in living, is that person himself. It would seem prudent to avoid offering information about other people's life situations unless it is directly asked for by the client and then only tentatively. The temptation is often great to suggest to clients what we ourselves think they should do. Or perhaps we offer them suggestions as to what we would do given their predicament. Such advice is not usually helpful but fortunately, rarely dangerous, as it is so rarely taken! It would seem that people are relatively self-protecting in this respect and that they do not accept advice that they cannot usefully use. On the other hand, this may be a reflection on the way in which clients choose the people they seek out to be counselled by. Sartre (1973) argued that one person goes to another for advice readily knowing the sort of advice that they will receive. They may not do this consciously, but it would seem that this process of selection does take place at some deeper level.

Informative counselling, then, is best restricted to relatively concrete situations, where expert information can make a direct contribution to the person's wellbeing. We have noted that this is rarely the case when it comes to other people's emotional and life problems: better and more effective methods of counselling exist and the skills involved in those methods are easily learned.

Informative counselling in practice

Sarah is a physiotherapist who is visiting an elderly patient, Joan Andrews, in the ward prior to her having an operation for a hip replacement. During the process of being taught breathing exercises, Joan asks Sarah about her operation. Sarah uses client-centred counselling interventions (see Chapter 7) to establish what Joan has and has not been told about her coming operation. She is then able to offer clear and precise information regarding what may be expected, being careful not to use jargon nor to 'talk down' to Joan. In this way, Joan's anxieties are relieved and she is better prepared for her operation because of her increased knowledge. There is evidence to suggest that patients who are given sufficient information about surgery and its possible outcomes suffer subjectively less pain than do those patients who are not prepared in this way (Haywood, 1975). In this example, too, the information given is of a concrete and practical nature that will enhance the patient's comfort and relieve her anxiety.

Educational counselling

Health professionals are often to be found working in an educational setting. Most of the professions engage people trained in those professions as educators to the next generation. A number of the caring professions, including nursing, operate an apprenticeship type of training, in which work in the field is combined with blocks of academic study. People who work in an educational capacity frequently find themselves in the role of personal tutor to one or more students. Such tutoring combines both the educational aspect of the student's life and also the personal. It is this dual function that can combine both types of counselling discussed previously – the supportive and the informative. It is usually useful, however, to establish some parameters to the student/tutor relationship and the use of a **contract** is helpful here.

In contract-setting, the tutor negotiates the following with the student:

1. the amount of time that they will spend together (e.g. 1 hour per week)
2. the type of counselling relationship that is required (e.g. academic and course-related and/or personal)
3. whether or not some of the academic counselling will take place in the context of a small group to include other personal tutees.

Clearly, there are occasions on which the personal aspects of a student's life will shade into their academic life. On the other hand, to keep a counselling conversation focused on one or other of these topics can enable both tutor and student to clarify what it is they want from the relationship at that particular time. Hopefully, too, the distinction can enable some objectivity about a student's academic work to be maintained by the tutor. When personal issues are discussed alongside academic issues, the problem of how to assess written and project work can become difficult as the tutor is too distracted by the personal issues that are involved.

Counselling in crisis

Another aspect of counselling is helping the person who suddenly finds himself in crisis. Murgatroyd and Woolfe (1982) have characterized a crisis in the following ways:

1. Symptoms of stress – the person experiences stress both physically and psychologically;
2. Attitude of panic or defeat – the person feels overcome by the situation and experiences both helplessness and hopelessness;
3. Focus on relief – the person wants, more than anything else, relief from the feeling of being in crisis;
4. Lowered efficiency – in other areas of their life, apart from the crisis, the person's functioning may be impaired;
5. Limited duration – because the experience is psychologically painful, it does not last long and can be viewed as an acute experience of limited duration.

Clearly, there are many different types of crises that occur in people's lives, ranging from sudden death in the family, to critical marital or relationship difficulties. Differences occur, too, with regard to the point at which an individual perceives himself as being in crisis. Thus, the point at which counselling intervention is offered will vary from person to person. Sometimes that intervention is offered through access to a crisis intervention team of one sort or another. Usually such teams are multidisciplinary and thus offer the services of a range of practitioners. At other times, crisis counselling is offered through telephone counselling and through a range of helplines. Clearly, telephone counselling calls for a very different range of skills than does face-to-face counselling in that the immediate presence of the person in distress is missing. In such a situation, all nonverbal means of communication between the two people are lost and verbal intervention is almost the only means of interchange available. The word almost is used consciously here, for even on the telephone, an intuitive sense of a situation may be grasped by the effective counsellor.

Crisis counselling calls for swift action in helping the person to restore their ability to function effectively. Schwartz (cited by Murgatroyd, 1986) offers some suggestions as to how such action may be initiated. Amongst other things, Schwartz suggests the following steps that the counsellor may take:

1. Help the person face up to the crisis – discourage denial and attempt to help them to be objective;
2. Break up the crisis into manageable doses – most people can deal with serious problems more easily if they are not overwhelmed by the sheer magnitude of the situation;
3. Avoid false reassurance – the counsellor should resist the temptation to prematurely assure the person in crisis that 'everything will work out OK';
4. Help and encourage the person to help themselves – if the person in crisis can actively use the help of friends or family this will cut down the dependence on the counsellor and increase independent decision-making;
5. Teach the person in crisis coping skills – once the immediate danger has past, the individual needs to develop a repertoire of coping strategies to help ward off future and similar situations.

Clearly, crisis counselling is demanding work and the urgency of the situation often calls for quick decisions to be made. In such situations it is easy to take over too quickly and for the counsellor to try to take control of the situation. Whilst this may help in the first instance, such an approach does not help the person in crisis in the longer term. Sometimes, crisis counselling calls for considerable constraint on the part of the counsellor and often it is emotionally draining. For this reason, it is often helpful, wherever possible, for crisis counselling to be conducted in pairs or by a small group of people. In this way, mutual support is offered by the counsellors to each other and more objective help is offered to the client.

Examples of crises that health professionals may have to help their patients or clients through are many and a short list of examples of such crises would include, at least, the following:

1. sudden death of a partner or spouse
2. sudden death of a child
3. serious and acute illness in the family
4. trauma caused by accident or injury
5. sudden onset of acute psychological or emotional distress
6. suicide or attempted suicide
7. fear of death or the process of dying
8. fear of surgical intervention
9. acute anxiety about the future

Counselling in spiritual distress

Spiritual distress is the result of total inability to invest life with meaning. It can be demotivating, painful and can cause anguish to the sufferer. Counselling people who experience such distress presents a considerable challenge to health professionals who care for them.

It would seem that the need to find meaning in what we do is a very basic human need (Bugental and Bugental, 1984). Such meaning may be framed in the context of a set of religious beliefs that can take very varied forms (Wallis, 1984). Alternatively, meaning may be found through adherence to a particular ideological viewpoint: philosophical, psychological, sociological or political. Others take the view expressed by Kopp (1974) that there is no meaning to life except what we as individuals invest in it. Those with a positivistic scientific view of the world may dismiss the metaphysical altogether and thus the notion of a spiritual problem does not arise for them.

The first qualification for engaging in spiritual counselling may be the development of an understanding of a wide range of religious doctrines, philosophical and political systems of thought and an appreciation of how various thinkers throughout history have approached the ultimate questions of life. Such an enterprise can be humbling. It can enable us to understand that not everyone views the world as we do and may guard against any temptation on the part of the counsellor to proselytize. As Jung pointed out (Fordham, 1966), the counsellor needs to be a 'wise' person, not only trained in counselling methods but also widely read, experienced and open-minded.

Counsellors also need, perhaps, a highly developed intuitive sense: the ability to see and understand beyond the words that people use to attempt to express themselves. Carl Rogers noted that he felt himself to be functioning best as a counsellor when he paid full attention to this intuitive sense (Rogers, 1967). Counselling in the spiritual domain, then, is far more than the development of a range of counselling skills. It involves the whole person and can, at times, tax the counsellor's own belief and value system. Indeed, the counsellor must be prepared to 'live on the edge' when counselling in spiritual distress and acknowledge that there are times when there are no answers to the taxing problems of meaning.

Who, then, are the people likely to require spiritual counselling? The range of those who experience spiritual problems is wide and includes adolescents suffering from identity crises (Erikson, 1959) to those in middle age who may suddenly be faced with the difficulty of individuation (Storr, 1983) to the older person who may fear death. Along this age dimension are those of any age who suddenly find themselves confronting the issue of personal meaning. This may happen as part of a depressive illness but it may also happen when depression is not present. Dispiritedness, or the failure to find meaning has been described as a state of mind separate to depression and identified as the questioning of the point of life in someone who is otherwise functioning 'normally' (Tillich, 1952; Bugental, 1980). It may occur, for instance, in the person who up to that point has held well-defined religious beliefs but who now has doubts about them. It can happen in those who are faced by some sort of extreme challenge in life and are left questioning the reasons for such an occurrence. It can occur, also, as a result of the crisis described in the previous section and should be looked for as a possibility after the immediate crisis has abated. Clearly, it can occur in a great number of situations that are found in hospitals: during sudden, severe and life-threatening illness; following surgical intervention that causes changes in body image (mastectomy, for example), following the death of a child or a close relative and numerous other situations in which the person may call into question the issue of meaning.

In later life, the problem of individuation described by Jung (Storr, 1983) as the quest for finding and understanding the self, may be preceded by a feeling of vacuum, pointlessness and lack of ability to be self-motivated. The psychoanalyst, Victor Frankl, has described this feeling as an 'existential vacuum' (Frankl, 1959; 1969; 1975). He argues that this is characterized by despair, distress and a feeling of emptiness. Frankl is clear, however, that this is not a neurotic condition but a very common human experience. Indeed, such a feeling is well described in works of literature that are concerned with the human condition. It occurs in the hero of Sartre's *Nausea* (1965) and Hesse's *Steppenwolf* (1927) and is addressed extensively in Colin Wilson's survey of such literature, *The Outsider* (Wilson, 1955). It is the darker side of the human situation.

The whole issue of dispiritedness, existential vacuum or spiritual collapse presents a great challenge to the health professional who meets people suffering from such life crises. How, then, may the practitioner answer such a challenge? How may she counsel the person, who, almost by definition, seems beyond counselling? Perhaps the first thing that she can do is to **listen** to the person. It is tempting when we are threatened by the content of another person's conversation to refuse to let them talk. Somehow, the despairing content of their conversation seems to call into question our own beliefs about life. This may indeed be the case and it suggests that before we engage in counselling of any sort, we therefore clarify our own belief and value systems (Simon *et al.*, 1978). If we are clearer about our own view of life, we may find that we are less threatened by the views of others. There is, however, no guarantee. We enter into every spiritual-counselling situation as something of an act of faith: there can be no absolute certainty that we will not be changed by the encounter. It may be important that this is the case. If we are so secure in our own belief system, we may also become closed minded and less questioning: such a position is probably not the best one from which to work as a counsellor.

Apart from listening to the person who is experiencing spiritual distress, we need also to **accept** what they say, if someone expresses particularly negative thoughts, the temptation is to try to persuade them to think otherwise. In counselling, however, the aim is to listen and to accept and not to argue. Often this means that the person being counselled needs to quietly talk through something, sit in silence for some time and generally to acknowledge and face the blankness that they feel. It is often the case that the very facing of the blankness can lead to an apparent paradoxical change. It is as though through allowing and accepting the feeling, the feeling itself changes. Sometimes those who face complete meaninglessness, find meaning. This accent on accepting rather than fighting feelings is described in detail by Reibel (1984) who calls it the homeopathic approach to counselling. She adopts the metaphor of homeopathy to describe this process of 'allowing' a condition or state of mind rather than fighting it. In homeopathic medicine, small doses of the toxins that cause an illness may be given as a remedy for the illness. So, in homeopathic counselling, the thoughts and feelings that are troubling the spiritually distressed person are encouraged rather than argued against. Sometimes by such encouragement the dispirited feelings are transformed or transmuted and replaced by more positive, life-asserting feelings.

Closely allied to this homeopathic approach is that which involves the use of paradoxical strategies. These are variously described as paradoxical intention (Frankl, 1960; 1975; 1978), paradoxical interventions (Tennen *et al.*, 1981) and paradoxical therapy (Fay, 1976; 1978). These constitute a cluster of techniques whose essential element is an unexpected reversal of the anticipated procedure. Thus, instead of joining forces with the client to tackle his dispiritedness, the practitioner suggests a continuance or even an intensification of the negative feelings. This curious about-turn in counselling can, again, sometimes encourage a contrary alleviation of the negative feelings. It is as though by being implored to get worse, the client gets better! On the other hand, such an approach will not work with everyone, nor will it suit every practitioner. It is, however, an approach that may be considered as one more means of helping the distressed person.

This is, perhaps, the crux of spiritual counselling and, for that matter, of any sort of counselling – that no one approach works for everyone. Health professionals engaged in spiritual counselling need to remain sensitive to personal needs and differences. Indeed, if they can develop the deeper listening approach alluded to previously and described in more detail in Chapter 5, they may enter the client's world view and discover, through the client, the right approach. The client, in other words, is telling the counsellor what help he needs. The difficulty lies in being receptive to that description. There are times when clients have great difficulty in articulating what their needs are, but such articulation is nearly always possible given time and sensitivity and also a considerable amount of humility on the part of the counsellor.

Health professionals acting as counsellors always need to know their limitations. They need to know when to call in other help agents, whether those agents are doctors, clergy, other members of the family or other health professionals. There are times, too, when counsellors have too close a relationship with the client and find their own judgement clouded by this closeness. If they are supported by other colleagues, such a period can be worked through to the benefit of both client and counsellor.

The skills involved in counselling the person who is spiritually distressed may serve as a template for the sorts of skills required in all counselling situations. Perhaps because of the extreme nature of the person's feelings, counselling in this situation calls upon certain aspects that we shall encounter again and again in later chapters – the ability to listen, to accept and to have some self-understanding.

It should be noted, too, that the word spiritual used in this context, is not necessarily synonymous with the word religious. Spiritual concerns, as they are described here, are concerns about **meaning**. The quest for meaning is probably a universal one and is just as much the domain of agnostics and atheists as it is of believers.

Counselling in spiritual distress in practice

Sian is a senior nurse in a large psychiatric hospital. Whilst talking to Ann, a ward sister, during her staff-appraisal meeting, she discovers that Ann finds it difficult to sustain interest in her work as person in charge of an acute-admissions ward. At first, this lack of motivation appears to be a result of having worked on the ward for two years. After further discussion, however, Ann talks of her difficulty in seeing the 'point' of her work and talks of a general disenchantment with life itself. Sian and Ann meet regularly and Ann is allowed to talk through her feelings. Gradually, she discovers a sense of purpose again, although there are times when both Sian and Ann are uncertain about the possible outcome of their discussions. Sian notes, too, that earlier in her career as a psychiatric nurse, she would have tended to dismiss Ann's problems as symptoms of depression.

Counselling in emotional distress

Frequently, there are times when the counselling relationship can evoke emotion in the client. Sometimes this occurs out of the discussion that the client is having – the very nature of the material under discussion is painful and brings to the surface a great deal of bottled-up feelings. At other times, the client comes to the practitioner in distress.

In the first instance, when the client is stirred up by the nature of the discussion, the most helpful thing that the counsellor can do appears to be to **allow** the full expression of those feelings (Heron, 1977a). As we have seen in the previous section, this allowing goes

15

against the cultural grain. We are more readily moved to cheer the person up or to help him to stop expressing strong feeling, even more so when that person's expression of emotion stirs up feelings in us as counsellors. It is arguable, however, that it is exactly because the person has been encouraged to bottle things up that they perceived themselves as having problems. It is as though the bottled-up emotion changes the person's perception and tends to make for more negative perceptions. On the other hand, if those emotions are fully released, the person's perception of the situation will often change to the more positive. Clearly, this is not always the case. People in all walks of life experience real and distressing situations that cannot easily be resolved: death in the family, unemployment, illness, financial problems and so forth. None of these situations can be changed easily by the process of counselling. Even though this is true, the individual's perception of their situation can still change through counselling and, in this case, through expression of pent-up emotion. In a sense, there are no good or bad life situations: what is good and bad is the way that we view those situations – the sense we make of them. Whilst counselling may not be able to halt the fact of much of life being intractable, it can help in encouraging a more positive and life-assertive world view.

In the situation where the client comes to the practitioner in a distressed and emotional state, a decision has to be made as to whether to distract that person and move them away from their emotional release or whether to accept the release as outlined previously. Much will depend here on what the client is asking of the counsellor. Is he asking for help to control his emotional state? Is he asking that the counsellor hear him and allow him his expression? As we noted in the section on counselling in spiritual distress (p. 11), the counsellor must learn to read the signs and to hear what is being requested. If there is still ambiguity and the client's needs and wants are not clear, the counsellor has the option of asking the client what he wants. At first, this may seem like an uncomfortable option. In practice, it is quite possible to say to the other person, 'Do you want to continue crying or would you like me to help you stop?' Again, such an intervention is counter-cultural. Normally we do not ask such questions! The question can do much to help the client to determine exactly what is needed at this particular time. It is easy to imagine that because a person is crying, they are out of control in every other respect. The person who is crying is still able to be self-determining and still able to make decisions about what it is they do or do not want of another person.

The specific skills involved in helping the person who is experiencing emotional release are described in Chapter 7. This section has merely opened up the question of what to do when someone is in emotional distress. Again, it would seem, the accepting method has much to commend it as a style of counselling.

THE RANGE OF COUNSELLING INTERVENTIONS

Whatever sort of counselling is undertaken, certain skills and processes are involved. Counselling skills can be divided into two groups:

1. listening and attending
2. verbal-counselling interventions

In other words, the counsellor listens to the client and verbally responds. The skills involved in listening are described more fully in Chapter 6. It may be useful, however, to identify the range of counselling interventions that may be used in any counselling situation. John Heron, a British philosopher and humanistic therapist has devised a valuable division of all possible therapeutic interventions called 'Six category intervention analysis' (Heron, 1986). The analysis transcends any particular theoretical stance adopted by the counsellor and has many applications. The six categories described in Heron's analysis are as follows:

1. prescriptive interventions
2. informative interventions
3. confronting interventions
4. cathartic interventions
5. catalytic interventions
6. supportive interventions

These six categories will be described in further detail but it is important to note that Heron further subdivides the categories into those he calls authoritative (the first three) and those he calls facilitative (the second three). Authoritative counselling interventions are those in which the counsellor plays a directive role in the counselling relationship and guides it in a fairly structured way. Facilitative counselling interventions are those in which the counsellor plays a less directive role and enables the client to take

17

more control over the relationship. Another way of describing the difference is that authoritative interventions are 'I tell you' interventions and facilitative ones are 'you tell me' interventions. Heron argues that the skilled counsellor is one who can use a balance of the two types of interventions appropriately and skilfully in a wide range of counselling situations. It is not, then, a question of using all of the different types of interventions in all counselling situations but of consciously choosing the right intervention for the right occasion. What, then, are examples of the six categories of therapeutic intervention?

Prescriptive interventions

Prescriptive interventions are those in which the counsellor's intention is to suggest or recommend a particular line of action. Thus, if the counsellor says 'I recommend you talk this over with your family', she is making a prescriptive intervention. Heron suggests that when prescriptive interventions are clumsily used, they can degenerate into heavy-handed, moralistic patronage. Certainly they can be overused in counselling, very easily.

Examples of how prescriptive interventions may be effective in the health-care setting are when a physiotherapist offers a recently paralysed person practical suggestions as to how he may increase his mobility with the use of a wheelchair, or offers the elderly person advice about how to correctly use a walking frame.

Informative interventions

Informative interventions are those in which the counsellor informs or instructs the client in some way. If, for example, the health professional says 'You will probably find that you will have some discomfort in your leg for about three weeks', she is using an informative intervention. Heron notes here, that unskilful use of informative interventions leads to dependence on the counsellor and the relationship can degenerate into the counselling situation becoming one of overteaching on the part of the counsellor. As we have seen from the previous discussion on informative counselling, information is best limited to concrete situations and should not extend to 'putting your life right' information.

The nurse who instructs a patient to complete a course of

antibiotics is offering informative help. It is notable that such information is limited to concrete, practical issues. As we have noted, it is easy to take over a patient's life and create dependence through offering too much information.

Confronting interventions

Interventions of this sort are those that challenge the client in some way or draw their attention to a particular type of repetitive behaviour. An example of a confronting intervention may be 'I notice that you frequently complain about the way your wife talks to you. . .'. If confrontation is used too frequently in the counselling situation, it may be perceived by the client as an aggressive approach. Clearly, confrontation needs to be used appropriately and sensitively. This issue is addressed more specifically in Chapter 9.

Cathartic interventions

These are interventions that enable the client to release tension through the expression of pent-up emotion. Thus an intervention that allows a person to cry may be termed a cathartic intervention. The counsellor may give the client permission to cry by saying 'You seem to be near to tears. . . it's alright with me if you cry. . .'. Cathartic interventions may be misused when they force the client to release feelings when that person is clearly not ready or willing to express them. It is sometimes tempting but rarely appropriate to anticipate that it will 'do the client good' to express bottled-up feeling. More appropriately, perhaps, it should be the client who decides when and if such release of emotion occurs. The issue of emotional release and cathartic skills are discussed in greater detail in Chapter 8.

There are very many situations in health care when effective use of cathartic skills is valuable. A short list would include, at least, the following:

1. supporting the recently bereaved person
2. helping the person who is adjusting to new, yet profound, disability
3. assisting people to cope with shock after trauma
4. helping the person to express their feelings after assault, rape or accident

19

5. enabling the depressed person to release pent-up feelings of anger or self-doubt

All carers need cathartic skills and yet, perhaps, they are the most difficult to develop. They require considerable self-awareness on the part of the professional and a willingness to explore our own emotional make-up.

Catalytic interventions

Catalytic interventions are those that draw the client out and encourage him to discuss issues further. Thus, any sort of questions are examples of catalytic interventions. Again, used inappropriately, questions can appear interrogative and intrusive. They need to be well timed and sensitively phrased. Certain other forms of catalytic intervention may be more appropriate than questions and these are discussed further in Chapter 7.

Catalytic interventions are perhaps the most useful of all interventions to the health professional. Often it is essential to explore how much a patient or client knows about his condition, prior to offering further information. The person skilled in catalytic counselling can discretely and tactfully help the person to express his own wants and needs. Thus, catalytic counselling can become an integral part of health-care **assessment**.

Supportive interventions

These are interventions that support, validate or encourage the client in some way. Thus, when the counsellor tells the client 'I appreciate what you are doing', they are offering a supportive intervention. Used badly, supportive interventions can degenerate into patronage. Often, too, they are symptomatic of the counsellor's need to too quickly reassure the client – perhaps evidence of the counsellor being a 'compulsive helper'.

These, then, are short descriptions of the six categories. Heron (1986) suggests that they are exhaustive, as a set of categories, of all possible therapeutic interventions. Thus, anything a counsellor can say to a client will fit under one of those six headings.

The category analysis has a number of applications. First, it can help us to appreciate a wide range of possible interventions to use in the counselling relationship. In everyday conversation, we tend to limit ourselves to a particular and often rather limited range of expressions, questions and verbal responses. The category analysis offers the chance to identify other interventions that we could use. Further, we can learn to make use of what Heron (1977b) calls 'conscious use of self'. In other words, we learn to take responsibility for what we say and choose to make a particular intervention at a particular time. At first, this obviously feels unnatural and clumsy. It is, however, the key to becoming an effective and appropriate counsellor. If we do not reflect on what we say and how we say it, we limit our competence. If we consciously choose what we say, then we stand to broaden our repertoire.

Second, the analysis can make us aware of alternative interventions. There are occasions in counselling, as in every other situation in life, where it is possible to think, 'What do I say now?' Reference to the category analysis offers further possibilities of response: this must be the case if Heron's claim that it is exhaustive of all possible therapeutic interventions is valid.

Further, the analysis can be used as a means of evaluating current intervention skills. The reader is asked to consider the six categories and to identify the two categories that are used most skilfully, at the present time and the two categories that are used least skilfully. In this way it is possible to determine areas in which you need further training or practice. This application of the analysis has wider implications, too, for the design of counselling-skills workshops and peer-support groups. Members of such groups can use the six categories to produce a collective group profile of skills and deficits. Out of this profile can emerge the content of a skills-development programme. The group can concentrate its efforts on those interventions that most people in the group identify as lacking. A method for using the analysis in a group context is described in the final chapter of this book.

The analysis can also be used as a research tool for identifying how groups of people view their own counselling skills. In a recent study of 93 trained nurses in the UK who were asked to rate themselves on their own perception of their levels of counselling skills using the analysis, most said that they were most effective at being prescriptive, informative and supportive, not as skilled at being catalytic and least skilled at using confronting and cathartic interventions effectively (Burnard and Morrison, 1987). Such research is easily carried out and can be used, at a local level, to determine training needs in the interpersonal domain, in much the same way as has been recommended above.

Becoming aware of the range of counselling skills available is the first step towards becoming an effective counsellor. The next stage is to consider when and how to use those skills effectively.

THE OUTCOME OF EFFECTIVE COUNSELLING

Clearly, different people respond differently to being counselled but it is worth considering what Carl Rogers noted was the general outcome of effective counselling. His list of the changes that may take place are based on observation and evaluation of numerous people 'getting better' in counselling and may serve as a useful indicator of the personal changes that can be achieved:

> The person comes to see himself differently. He accepts himself and his feelings more fully. He becomes more self-confident and self-directing. He becomes more flexible, less rigid in his perceptions. He adopts more realistic goals for himself. He behaves in a more mature fashion. . . He becomes more accept-ant of others. He becomes more open to the evidence, both to what is going on outside of himself and to what is going on inside of himself. He changes in his basic personality characteristics in constructive ways.
>
> (Rogers, 1967)

2

Psychological approaches to counselling

Anyone who acts as a counsellor does so from a position of having certain assumptions about the nature of the person. We all carry with us a certain set of beliefs about the psychological make-up of ourselves and other people. Often this belief system is only hazily articulated. Sometimes it is not articulated at all. However vague that system is, it motivates us and helps us in our decision-making about how to help other people. In this chapter, some formalized belief systems about the person are briefly explored, drawn from a variety of schools of psychology. It is suggested that in exploring this variety of approaches to the person, we may be able to clarify our own set of beliefs. It is only through clarifying what we believe that we can hope to change or modify our practice. What follows, then, is a brief exploration of some psychological approaches to counselling. Some will seem to be congruent with what we believe ourselves. Others will seem quite alien. The skill may be to try to adopt the psychological approach least like our own and to suspend judgement on it for a while. In trying out a new set of ideas in this way, we are already developing a skill that is vital in the process of counselling – that of adopting a frame of reference different to our own. This is a process that is fundamental to counselling. As we listen to the other person, we must try to enter their view of the world and temporarily make it our own in order to understand that person. So too, perhaps, it will be useful to enter a theoretical approach that is different to our own in order to try to understand it.

There is also a practical reason for adopting this approach. As we sit with a client, reflecting upon what they say in terms of the belief system we have about the nature of persons, so they, too, sit with their own belief system about the nature of the person. Clearly, there is no reason to suppose that the belief system that the client has, however hazy or well articulated, will correspond to our own. We cannot guarantee that the client has the same set of views about human nature that we do. It is important, then, to consider a range of ways of making sense of human beings and a range of ways of allowing theory to inform our practice. What follows does not claim to be an exhaustive classification of all possible views of the person, but will allow the individual reader to draw his or her own conclusions about why people may do the things they do and how best to help them in the counselling situation. The discussion here of the various approaches is necessarily brief and the reader is referred to the considerable literature on the topic for a more detailed exposition. The bibliography at the end of this book offers a variety of sources of further information.

THE PSYCHODYNAMIC APPROACH

Sigmund Freud is usually viewed as the father of the psychodynamic school of psychology (Hall, 1954). Essential to the approach is the notion that people are, to a greater or lesser extent, affected by unconscious motives and drives. That is to say, we cannot clearly give an account of why we are behaving, thinking or feeling as we are, at any given time, because there are forces at work beneath the level of conscious awareness that cause us to act in a particular way. This unconscious level of the mind is developed out of experiences that happened to us in earlier parts of our lives that we were unable to deal with at the time. When we encounter an experience in the present that is in any way similar to that past event, we experience anxiety – we are unconsciously reminded of the situation.

For psychodynamic psychologists, then, the key to understanding a person's present behaviour is through a thorough exploration of their past. Thus, the psychodynamically oriented counsellor will usually choose to explore the client's past history and help him to identify and, if necessary, to relive various painful, past events in order to make him less anxious and more able to make rational decisions about the present. In essence, then, the psychodynamic approach is a deterministic one. **Determinism** is the notion that every event has a cause and in this case, every aspect of a person's behaviour has a cause and that cause is buried in the person's personal history. If you want to understand the person in the present, you must first understand his past. Essentially, too, a person's behaviour is basically understandable once these links to the past have been made. The process of counselling from the psycho-dynamic point of view may be likened to a jigsaw. Once all the pieces are put together, the whole thing makes sense. It is notable that many health professionals, particularly those in social work and certain types of nursing may have been 'brought up' on the psycho-dynamic way of understanding people. It may be useful for them to explore other ways.

The psychodynamic approach in practice

The health professional who adopts the psychodynamic approach to counselling will tend to:

1. highlight the relationship between past and present life events
2. acknowledge that unconscious forces are at work that affect the client's behaviour
3. encourage the expression of pent-up emotion

Examples of practical applications of this approach in the health-care field include:

1. helping with long-term emotional problems
2. coping with anxiety
3. helping the client who talks of having had an unhappy childhood

THE BEHAVIOURAL APPROACH

While Freud was developing his theories in Europe around the turn of the century, John Watson in the USA was developing a different and opposing view of the person (Murphy and Kovach, 1972). He was adamant that the study of the person should be a scientific enter-prise. To that end, he felt it should abandon the introspective methods suggested by Freud and concentrate on the arguably more objective study of human behaviour. Developing this theme, Watson argued that all human behaviour was learned and therefore could, if necessary, be unlearned. Such learning took place through the process he called **positive reinforcement**. Essentially, we learn those behaviours that we get encouraged to learn and forget those behaviours for which no such encouragement is forthcoming. For the behavioural counsellor, then, the important issue is not the recollec-tion of painful, past events but the identification of what the client sees as undesirable behaviours. Once those undesirable (or uncomfortable) behaviours have been identified, the next step is to organize a scheme whereby more positive behaviours will be encouraged (or, in behavioural terms, a 'schedule of reinforcement' is drawn up). The client is then encouraged to go away and work at developing the desired behaviours through the scheme organized with the counsellor. No attempt is made, in the behavioural approach, to understand the cause of behaviours in terms of the past as no such theory of causation is mooted.

The behavioural approach may be described as a **mechanistic** approach in that it tends to view the person as a highly complex machine – perhaps rather like a computer. And just as a computer responds only to its programming, so the person responds only to the learning he has achieved through reinforcement. The key issues in the behavioural approach, then, are learning, unlearning and relearning. The behavioural approach is frequently used as basis for the training of psychiatric nurse–therapists.

The behavioural approach in practice

The health professional who adopts the behavioural approach to counselling will tend to:

1. set practical aims and objectives in counselling
2. discuss **behaviour** rather than reasons for patterns of behaviour
3. identify a practical programme of small changes that the client will be able to achieve in order to cope with problems of living

Examples of practical applications of this approach in the health-care field include:

1. dealing with long-term behaviour problems
2. helping with behaviour problems in children
3. enabling clients to cope with bereavement

THE HUMANISTIC APPROACH

In the late 1940s and 1950s and perhaps reaching a peak in the 1960s, a movement began in psychology in America that challenged the determinism of psychodynamic psychology and the mechanism of behavioural psychology (Shaffer, 1978). This was what came to be

26

known as the 'third force' in psychology – humanistic psychology. Drawing heavily on the field of existential philosophy, humanistic psychology argued that people were essentially free and responsible for their own condition. They were neither 'driven' by an unconscious mind nor were they only a product of what they had learned. Essentially they were **agents**. The fact of consciousness gave them the ability to determine their own course of action through life and they were the best arbiters of what was and what was not good for them. In humanistic psychology there could be no 'grand plan' of how people's minds work or how their behaviour could be manipulated. Humanistic psychology stressed individuality and individual differences in the human condition.

It was out of the humanistic school that the client-centred approach to counselling developed (Rogers, 1951). Rogers consistently argued that what made for effective counselling was trusting the individual's ability to find his own way through his problems. Rogers believed to this end that people were essentially life-asserting and 'good', by nature. In this respect, he drew from the philosopher Rousseau and, perhaps more directly from the American pragmatist and philosopher of science, John Dewey (1916; 1938). The aim of counselling for Rogers, then, was not necessarily to explore the person's past nor to necessarily try to modify their behaviour but to accept them and to help them to progress through their difficulties by their own route. Counsellors, then, were not experts in other people's problems but individuals who accompanied other people on their search for personal meaning. The client-centred approach has been pervasive in the counselling world and has been adopted as a starting point for many training courses for counsellors and used in a variety of contexts in the health professions in the UK, from psychiatric nurse training (ENB, 1982) to the training of marriage guidance counsellors (MGC, 1983).

The humanistic approach in practice

The health professional who adopts the humanistic approach to counselling will tend to:

1. avoid 'interpreting' the client's behaviour
2. seek to encourage the client to identify his own solutions to his problems
3. acknowledge that every individual is to some degree responsible for his or her own behaviour

Examples of practical applications of this approach in the health-care field include:

1. dealing with spiritual distress and problems of meaning
2. helping with problems of self-image
3. helping to free the client who believes that he is somehow controlled by his circumstances

THE COGNITIVE APPROACH

The cognitive approach to counselling takes the view that what we think about ourselves affects the way we feel about ourselves. Thus, if we change our way of thinking, we can modify our feelings. Further, the argument is that many people hold exaggerated or incorrect beliefs about themselves that nevertheless affect their self-image. Examples of such false beliefs include 'No-one likes me', 'Everyone thinks I'm stupid' and 'I can't cope with anything'. These 'globalisms' or very general statements can have a negative effect on the person's functioning. The aim of the cognitive counsellor is to challenge these inaccurate and negative statements in order to modify the way the person thinks about himself and thus how he feels about himself.

Albert Ellis (1962), who developed 'rational emotive therapy', a particular sort of cognitive therapy, argued that there were twelve typical irrational beliefs that people could hold about themselves. They were not intended to be an exhaustive list of all the possible irrational beliefs that people can hold but represent commonly held erroneous beliefs that may have a profound effect on how a person thinks, feels and acts. The twelve beliefs that Ellis identified are:

1. It is a dire necessity that I be loved or approved of by everyone for everything I do;
2. Certain acts are wrong and evil and those who perform these acts should be severely punished;
3. It is terrible, horrible and catastrophic when things are not the way I would like them to be;
4. Unhappiness is caused by external events – it is forced upon one by external events, other people and circumstances;
5. If something is or may be dangerous or fearsome, I should be terribly concerned about it;
6. It is easier to avoid or replace life's difficulties than to face up

to them;

7. I need someone or something stronger or greater than myself upon which I can rely;
8. I should be thoroughly competent, adequate and achieving in all the things I do and should be recognized as such;
9. Because something in my past strongly affected my life, it should indefinitely affect it;
10. What other people do is vitally important to my existence and I should therefore make great efforts to change them to be more like the people I would like them to be;
11. Human happiness can be achieved by inertia and inaction;
12. I have virtually no control over my emotions and I just cannot help feeling certain things.

Ellis claimed that anyone who holds any one or more of these beliefs is likely to experience distress inasmuch as they affect the way that person acts on those beliefs. Clearly this is a contentious list, but it is interesting and perhaps salutary to reflect on it and to reflect on the degree to which we ourselves hold any of these beliefs!

In the cognitive approach, the style of counselling is one of challenging and confronting the client's belief system. In this respect, it is almost diametrically opposed to the style of counselling advocated by Carl Rogers – the client-centred approach. In the latter, the aim is to fully accept whatever the client says as a valid point of view about how that person views the world at that time. In the former approach, the aim is to call into question any number of beliefs that may be stopping the client from living fully and effectively. The approach has been used effectively with people who suffer from depression and other debilitating problems in living and practical examples of how the approach is used in practice are well described by Aaron Beck *et al.* (1979).

The cognitive approach in practice

The health professional who adopts the cognitive approach to counselling will tend to:

1. rely less on personal warmth and more on confrontation in the counselling relationship
2. use a logical and rational approach to problem-solving

3. encourage the client to develop a realistic and pragmatic outlook on life

Examples of practical applications of this approach in the health-care field include:

1. helping the person who is depressed
2. helping the person who has multiple problems
3. encouraging rational thinking in someone who is highly emotional

THE TRANSACTIONAL-ANALYSIS APPROACH

Transactional analysis offers an economical way of describing and discussing people's relationships with one another. Formulated by the American psychotherapist, Eric Berne (1964; 1972), the analysis suggests that we all relate to other people (and the world) from three distinct 'ego states'. These ego states are described as the Parent, the Adult and the Child. When we operate from the Parent (which is developed through the early absorption of parental and judgemental attitudes), we tend to talk down to others, feel superior to them or patronize them. On the other hand, when we operate from the Child (which is mainly developed through our experiences of being a child), we tend to adopt a subservient relationship *vis-à-vis* other people. Thus, we become dependent upon them or submit too readily to their demands and feel uncomfortable as a result. Berne argues that the most appropriate method of relating to others is through the Adult, which is to say that we meet others as mature, equal beings.

Beyond this first formulation, it is possible to map the ways in which people relate to one another from ego state to ego state. Thus a husband, for example, may relate to his wife from his Adult to her Child. Now if she is satisfied with this relationship, all well and good. Problems start, however, when the wife tries to relate to her husband on an Adult–Adult basis! This represents what Berne calls a 'crossed transaction' and will tend to lead to problems in the relationship (see Figures 2.1 and 2.2). The aim of transactional analysis is to enable clients to identify the sorts of relationship 'games' that they play with one another via these ego states and to learn to relate more readily on an Adult–Adult basis.

Figure 2.1 Example of an unequal but satisfactory transaction.

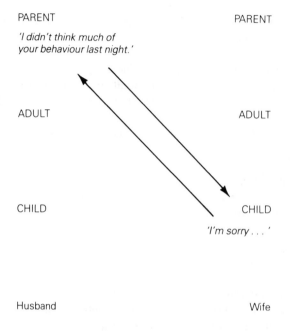

Figure 2.2 Example of an unequal and unsatisfactory transaction.

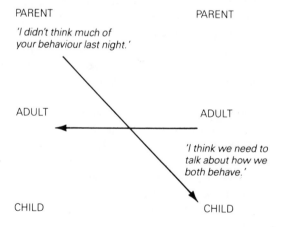

The transactional-analysis approach in practice

The health professional who adopts the transactional-analysis approach to counselling will tend to:

1. notice the interpersonal 'games' that people play
2. encourage the client to remain Adult in his relationships
3. encourage the client to try new strategies in his relationships

Examples of practical applications of this approach in the health-care field include:

1. marital and relationship difficulties
2. encouraging the client to become more assertive
3. identifying more adult ways of dealing with problems

THE PERSONAL-CONSTRUCT APPROACH

The personal-construct approach was developed by George Kelly (1955). Kelly used the metaphor of the scientist to describe how the person progresses through life. Thus, what we do is to predict how things will be in the near future (we develop a hypothesis). Then we test out that hypothesis in terms of what actually happens. As a result of what happens, we either consider our hypothesis confirmed or we discard it in favour of a revised hypothesis. Thus, according to Kelly, life is a series of personal predictions and confirmations or reconstructions. Our view of the world and of ourselves changes according to what happens to us and what sense we make of what happens to us.

Second, argues Kelly, we tend to view the world through a series of 'constructs' or 'ways of viewing' that colour our vision of how the world is. These constructs may be likened to a series of pairs of goggles that we put on at various times in order to make sense of what we perceive. An important point here, is that the 'goggles' that people wear are not inaccurate or accurate or right or wrong; they merely represent different aspects of the world that stand out or are important for us.

Kelly devised an interesting way of exploring people's personal constructs and the following activity demonstrates how such constructs or ways of seeing can be elicited. Try the exercise now.

An exercise to explore personal constructs

Think of three people that you know. Choose people from different aspects of your life. You may, for example, choose (a) someone you live with, (b) someone you know at work and (c) a close friend, though any three people will be fine. Now consider a way in which two of those people are similar and different to the third. This quality, behaviour or characteristic is what Kelly would call a **construct**. Now consider what you take to be the opposite of that quality, behaviour or characteristic. There are no right or wrong answers, but Kelly considers that this opposite characteristic represents another aspect of a person's construct system. Now consider to what degree you tend to view other people in terms of those two qualities, behaviours or characteristics.

You may like to try the activity again with a different trio of people and see what constructs you elicit in this case. If the process is repeated a number of times, you will tend to see a pattern of responses emerging. For Kelly, these represent something of your particular and idiosyncratic way of viewing the world.

It is important to say that no-one can interpret anything from your responses but they may give you some clarification as to what stands out about other people in your life experience.

For Kelly, then, the process of counselling can concern itself with exploring the ways in which the client construes the world around him. Gradually through such exploration, the person can come to modify or change their construct system in order to make their lives more liveable.

Personal-construct psychology views the person as an evolving, dynamic subject who is continuously modifying his view of the world in the light of what happens to him. Thus, as we have seen, that person may be likened to a scientist and the person's constructs as the set of criteria, rules or methods of interpretation through which that person modifies or changes his picture of the world. Epting (1984) and Stewart and Stewart (1981) offer practical methods of using the personal-construct approach in counselling.

The personal-construct approach in practice

The health professional who adopts the personal-construct approach to counselling will tend to:

1. acknowledge that people differ from one another in fundamental ways
2. look for the client's belief and value system as a clue to problem-solving
3. avoid interpreting the client's problems

Examples of practical applications of this approach in the health-care field include:

1. helping the client to enhance self-awareness
2. coping with marital and relationship difficulties
3. 'unpacking' complex and multifaceted problems

THE GESTALT-THERAPY APPROACH

The gestalt approach (it is usually spelt with a lower case 'g', perhaps to distinguish it from Gestalt Psychology – a different thing altogether!), was devised by Fritz Perls (1969) who drew from a number of influences, including psychoanalysis, phenomenology, existentialism and Eastern philosophy (Smith, 1975). The German world *gestalt* is not easily translatable but roughly corresponds to the notion of wholeness or completeness. The gestalt approach emphasizes the interplay between psychological or mental state and the state of the body, thus pointing up the totality of personal experience. It also concentrates on the changing and fluctuating nature of mental and physical state and concentrates most particularly on what is happening to the person now. It argues, reasonably, that the past is past and the future unknowable, therefore the focus of counselling attention should be the present moment. Thus, the gestalt approach encourages the client to become aware of what they are thinking, feeling and sensing, physically, in the here-and-now and how they restrict or limit themselves by making continuous reference to the past or how things may be in the future. Further, it uses a particular set of sometimes startling interventions to enable the client to explore various aspects of what is happening to them. As with the personal-construct and humanistic approaches, the emphasis is on the client interpreting or making sense of what is happening to them: it is not the counsellor's place to do that. The following dialogue may give something of the unique flavour of the gestalt approach.

Counsellor: What are you feeling at the moment?

Client: Nervous, odd.

Counsellor: Where in terms of your body do you feel that nervousness, oddness?

Client: (rubs his stomach)

Counsellor: Can you increase those feelings?

Client: Yes, but what a strange thing to ask! Yes, they're spreading up into my chest

Counsellor: And what are you feeling now?

Client: It's changing. . . I'm feeling angry now!

Counsellor: Who are you angry with?

Client: Me! I realize that I've been bottling up my feelings for months!

Counsellor: OK. . . Just imagine that your bottled-up feelings are sitting in that chair over there. . . what do you want to say to them?

Client: Go away! You stop me getting on with what I want to do!

Counsellor: And what do the feelings say back to you?

Client: I keep you in check! I stop you from getting too involved with people!

Counsellor: And what do you make of all that?

Client: How odd! I realize how much I restrict myself by holding on to everything – it's become convenient! I feel different again, now. . . something else is happening.

And so the dialogue continues. The counsellor's aim is to stay with the client's moment-to-moment phenomenology or perception of himself and to help him to explore it. As we have noted, the counsellor does not interpret what the client says nor offer suggestions as to how he may 'put his life right'. These are important principles in this person-centred and present-centred approach. Perls *et al.* (1951) offer a manual that, besides outlining the principles and theory of the gestalt approach, suggests a wide range of do-it-yourself gestalt exercises to increase self-awareness and clarify perception. A number of colleges and extra-mural departments of universities both in the UK and the USA offer short and extended courses in the gestalt approach.

The gestalt-therapy approach in practice

The health professional who adopts the gestalt-therapy approach to counselling will tend to:

1. treat each counselling situation as unique
2. deal with issues as they arise and in the here-and-now
3. notice small, nonverbal behaviours exhibited by the client

Examples of practical applications of this approach in the health-care field include:

1. helping the client who bottles up emotion
2. helping the person who has difficulty in verbalizing his problems
3. coping with problems of self-image and self-confidence

THE ECLECTIC APPROACH

In the end, what we do in counselling depends upon a number of issues: our skill levels, what we feel comfortable with doing in the counselling relationship, our belief and value systems as they relate to how we view what people are 'about', our level of self-awareness, our mood at the time, our present life situation, our perception of what (if anything) is wrong with the client, current work load and time available and many other factors. Thus it is reasonable to argue that no one set of counselling tools or no one particular approach can be appropriate in every counselling situation. What is perhaps more useful is that the health professional considers a wide range of possibilities, tries out some of the approaches (first, perhaps, with a willing colleague and in return, having that colleague try them out on the health professional!) and slowly incorporates the approaches that most suit that person into a personal repertoire. This personal repertoire or personal style offers the most flexible approach to counselling – the eclectic approach. Further, it is in line with Heron's argument in Chapter 1 (p. 20) that the counsellor becomes skilled in a wide range of possible counselling interventions in order to help a wide range of people. After all, health professionals meet a wide range of clients varying considerably in their cultural backgrounds, their personal experience, belief systems, needs, wants and wishes, political persuasions and personal psychologies. It is important that we offer clients what they want and not necessarily what we perceive that they want. The counselling relationship belongs to the client and not to the counsellor: we should not be dazzling them with a range of counselling interventions but finding out what they really want. In a sense, this is almost overwhelmingly simple, for as Epting notes, echoing the social psychologists, Allport, Kelly and others: 'If you want to know something about someone why not ask them: they might just tell you!' (Epting, 1984).

The eclectic approach in practice

The health professional who adopts the eclectic approach to counselling will tend to:

1. believe that no one approach to counselling suits each situation
2. read widely and learn a variety of different sorts of counselling skills
3. run the risk of being 'jack of all counselling skills and master of none'!

Examples of practical applications of this approach in the health-care field include:

1. everyday counselling practice
2. working with the client who does not respond to a particular counselling approach
3. helping the person who has very varied problems in living

PSYCHOLOGICAL APPROACHES TO COUNSELLING AND THE HEALTH PROFESSIONAL

As we have noted, no one school of psychology or theoretical approach to counselling offers *the* way of viewing the person. The approaches offer different ways of looking at the person and those ways of looking are not necessarily mutually exclusive. Which of the approaches the health professional chooses to use as a guide to understanding the process of counselling will depend on a number of factors, including, at least: her original psychological training that accompanied her basic professional training, the influences of any workshops, study days or further training, exposure to colleagues and friends who offer different points of view, further reading around the topic and so forth.

Another deciding factor may be the type of relationship that the health professional has with her client and the amount of time they spend together. The social worker, the speech therapist and the psychiatric nurse may all spend considerable time building up a relationship that, itself, may last for months or even years. On the other hand, the physiotherapist and the occupational therapist may form a shorter if quite intense relationship. It may be that the shorter relationships require a pragmatic psychology that allows for goals to be set and to be achieved: in this sense, the behavioural approach offers usable concepts that can help to structure the relationship. Or, if a longer term relationship is being developed, a 'process' model may be more applicable and the health-professional-as-counsellor may wish to consider those models that emphasize the quality of the relationship and an analysis of what is going on in that relationship. Here, the psychodynamic and humanistic approaches may help. In the end, too, what will determine what any health professional adopts as a psychological model for understanding the counselling relationship will depend on her own beliefs about the nature of people. In order to clarify what our beliefs are, we need to develop a degree of self-awareness – the topic of the following chapter.

3

Counselling and self-awareness

Self-awareness is an essential component in the counselling process. It is necessary for a number of reasons. These will be discussed first before the questions of self-awareness itself are addressed.

First, self-awareness allows us to discriminate between our own problems and those of the client. If we do not have at least minimal self-awareness, it is easy for us to identify with the other person's problems and to imagine that they are similar to, or even the same as, our own. The reverse of this situation is also possible. Without self-awareness it is possible to imagine that everyone else (and particularly this client) has the same problems as we do. In this way, our own problems are projected onto the client. We need to be able to identify clear 'ego boundaries': to make a clear distinction between ourselves and our client. As a matter of fact, what the client is describing at any particular time is never the same as a situation we have found ourselves in. It may be similar to it, but it can never be the same. Self-awareness can enable us to mark out our ego boundaries and successfully discriminate between what belongs to us and what belongs to the client. Haydn describes the problem well when he writes:

Day by day, hour by hour, we misunderstand each other because we cross well-marked boundaries; we blur the sense of *you out there* and me here; we merge, frequently very sloppily, the subjective with the objective, in various ways. We make of the other person simply an extension of self, either through the attribution of our own thoughts and attitudes to the other person, or by too facile a decision about his nature, after which we go on responding to him as though he were the character we invented.   (Haydn, 1965)

Such demarcation is also an essential part of the counsellor taking care of herself. When ego boundaries become blurred, considerable emotion is invested in the relationship by the counsellor and the net result can be **burnout** – emotional and physical exhaustion as a result of work-related stress. Burnout manifests itself in the following sorts of ways:

1. disillusionment with the job
2. a feeling of hopelessness and inability to cope
3. a need to get away from people
4. a loss of ability to empathize with others

Burnout can be prevented through reflection on our performance and through developing self-awareness as discussed below.

Secondly, self-awareness enables us to make what Heron (1977b) calls 'conscious use of the self'. Without awareness we will tend to feel that any counselling interventions we make are spontaneous and not offered consciously. Now, the point of conscious use of the self is that we learn to reflect on what is happening during the counselling relationship and we choose the interventions we make. In other words, the words and phrases that we use are intended and chosen consciously, rather than their just happening. Initially, such conscious use of the self can seem awkward and clumsy. We tend to be socialized into dividing human action up into natural (and therefore, presumably sincere) and contrived (and, therefore, presumably, insincere). The suggestion that we choose particular types of words or expressions smacks of unnaturalness and therefore tends to sound disagreeable.

On reflection, however, it may be noted that all other human skills, apart from listening and talking to others, are learned through the process of consciously considering what we are doing. If we are to become skilled as nurses, doctors or social workers, we must concentrate on what we do and observe the outcomes of our actions. The verbal skills of counselling can also be learned in a similar way and the concept of 'conscious use of self' has a variety of applications.

As we have already noted, in the first place, such use of the self can enable us to choose the right sort of counselling intervention for the right occasion. It can bring clarity and precision to the counselling relationship. If, for example, we use the category analysis identified in the previous chapter, we can choose to vary our repertoire of verbal interventions in a way that helps this particular person at this particular time. In this sense, then, conscious use of the self enhances sensitivity to the other person's needs.

Next, conscious use of the self can help us to distinguish between the client's problems and our own. In this way it serves to maintain and clarify the ego boundaries alluded to at the beginning of this chapter. In the process of developing conscious use of the self, we learn to notice ourselves and to pay attention to how we are reacting to the unfolding, counselling session. Such self-noticing can enable us, again, to make more sensitive use of our counselling interventions, be more tactful and truly meet the arising needs of the client. This process also has other connotations, for as Rollo May (1983b) notes, what the counsellor is feeling is often a direct reflection of what the client is feeling, once the counselling relationship deepens and becomes more intense. Thus, attention by the counsellor to her own changing feelings can help in the process of understanding and empathizing with the client.

The process of developing conscious use of self can be an uncomfortable one. Three stages in its development may be noted and these are described below.

First stage

In this stage, the person is unaware of the range of possible skills and interventions that are available to them. This is the stage of being natural or spontaneous. There is a tendency, in this stage, for the person to believe that people are 'born counsellors' and that the skills of counselling either come naturally to the individual or they cannot be developed at all. This may be called the unskilled stage.

Second stage

In the second stage of the process, the person becomes aware of the possible range of interventions available to her and feels clumsy as a result. It may be compared to the process of learning to drive a car. In the first place, we do not know how to drive the car at all. As we learn to drive, we have to pay attention to a wide range of different actions and the net result is that we are awkward and clumsy. So it is with the process of learning counselling through conscious use of the self. This may be called the clumsy stage.

Third stage

In the final stage of learning, the skills and interventions involved in counselling are absorbed by the person and they become skilled in counselling. Conscious use of the self has become a normal part of their repertoire of behaviour and no longer feels awkward or clumsy. Interestingly, too, the naturalness returns. The skills having been learned, emerge without forethought: the counsellor no longer has to consider what to say or what not to say but readily responds in the counselling situation out of the wide range of skills that have become her own. What remains conscious, however, is the ability to notice what is happening as the relationship unfolds. What has changed is the ability to act in an appropriate and sensitive manner whilst being guided by the observations made during this process of noticing. This may be called the skilled stage of counselling development.

NOTICING IN THE DEVELOPMENT OF COUNSELLING SKILLS

It will be noted that frequent reference will be made to the notion of **noticing**, of paying close attention to what is happening both in the counselling relationship and in the counsellor herself. This notion is a key one in the whole of the process of learning to become and learning to remain, a skilful and effective counsellor. It is also a central concept in the idea of self-awareness and one that will be referred to again in this context. Clearly, unless we notice what is happening to us, we cannot become self-aware. In exploring the notion of self-awareness as it applies to counselling, it will be useful, first, to consider the concept of the self.

The action of noticing can be readily used in any health-care setting. It is useful and instructive merely to notice our reactions to certain situations that occur. For instance, what do we notice about our own reactions to any of the following:

1. attempted suicide
2. severe incontinence in a young adult
3. severe and disfiguring handicap
4. the psychiatric patient admitted to a general ward

We may want to argue that, as professionals, we do not react to such human problems but we take action to help them. If this sort of argument is offered, it is worth listening a little closer to what is going on inside! It is easy for us to delude ourselves that we do not react to extreme aspects of human suffering as do other nonprofessionals. Again, it is salutary to question this stance and vital to do so if we are to become effective counsellors. We can never afford to become 'case-hardened' as carers or as counsellors.

THE SELF

The idea of what it means to have a self has been discussed down through the ages by philosophers, theologians, psychologists, sociologists, psychiatrists and political theorists. Psychologists have approached the concept from a variety of points of view. Some have tried to analyse out the factors that go to make up the self rather as a chemist might try to discover the chemicals that are present in a particular solution. Others have argued that there are certain consistent aspects of the self that determine, to some extent, the way in which we live our lives. Psychoanalytical theory, as we have seen, argues that early childhood experiences profoundly affect and shape the self, determining how, as adults, we react to the world. Childhood experiences, in this theoretical construction, lay the foundations of the self that may be modified by life experience but, nevertheless, stay with us throughout life. Such a view, as we noted on p. 24, is deterministic in that it argues that our present sense of self is determined by earlier life experiences and we are shaped, to a greater or lesser extent, by our childhoods.

Other psychological theorists argue that there are problems with reductionist theories – theories that attempt to analyse the self into discrete parts. Such theorists prefer to view the self from a holistic or gestalt perspective. This approach argues that the whole or totality of the self is always something more than the sum of the parts that go to make it up. Just as we cannot discover exactly what we like about a piece of music by examining it note by note, neither can we fully understand the self by compartmentalizing it. In this sense, then, the self can never completely be defined, for the subject of our study – the self – is always evolving and is always more than the sum of the parts.

It is worth noting, too, that we do not exist as selves-in-isolation. What we are and who we are depends, to a very considerable extent, on the other people with whom we live, work and relate. Our sense of self also depends upon how those other people define us, too. In this sense, other people are frequently telling us who we are. As health professionals, we rely on other colleagues, on clients and on friends offering us both positive and negative feedback on our performance as people. Such feedback is slowly absorbed by the individual, modifying and (hopefully) enhancing the sense of self.

It may be useful, then, to consider the range of aspects that go to make up a sense of self. As with any such analysis of self, it cannot hope to be exhaustive of all aspects of the self but it may serve to highlight the complex and multifaceted nature of the subject. Five aspects of self are considered here:

1. the physical self
2. the private self
3. the social self
4. the spiritual self
5. the-self-as-defined-by-others

The physical self

The physical self refers to the bodily or 'felt' sense of self. We are all (like it or not!) contained within a body and our perception of what we and other people think we look like contributes to how we see ourselves as a person. Further, there is an intimate link between how we feel psychologically and how we feel physically. To argue otherwise is to invoke the famous Cartesian split – the notion (propounded by the French philosopher, Descartes) that the body and the mind could be considered separately. The acknowledgement that the mind and body are so closely linked (and, arguably, the body 'produces' the mind) has considerable implications for counselling as we shall see in a later chapter. Suffice to say, here, that in noticing our 'body self' we may learn much about how we perceive ourselves generally. Noticing changing bodily sensations can be one route towards developing self-awareness.

The private self

The private self alludes to that part of us that we live inside – the hidden part of us that we reveal slowly – if at all – to other people. R.D. Laing has written a considerable amount on this concept (Laing, 1959) and suggested that it is quite possible for the 'private' self to watch the 'public' self in action! Certainly from the point of view of developing self-awareness, it is useful to become aware of this inner, private self and to notice to what degree and with whom that private sense of self is shared. Again, from the counselling point of view, such a notion of private self has considerable relevance, for it is that private self that is often shared in the counselling relationship.

The social self

The social self is that aspect of the person that is shared openly with others. It may be contrasted with the private self. It is the self that we choose to show to other people. The degree to which there is congruence between our private self and our social self may indicate our level of emotional and interpersonal security. Both Rogers (1951) and Laing (1959) have argued that when there is a close correspondence between the inner experience of self and the outer presentation of it, emotional security and stability tend to be present also. It is interesting and salutary to reflect on the degree to which this is true for us at the moment of reading this!

The spiritual self

The spiritual self refers to the aspect that is concerned with a search for personal meaning. As we noted in the first chapter, personal meaning may be framed within a variety of contexts: religious, philosophical, political, sociological, psychological and so forth. It is the spiritual aspect of the self that makes sense of what is happening to the person. It is that aspect of self concerned with belief and value systems. It may also be that part of the self that is concerned with the **transpersonal** aspects of being – that which unites all persons. Rogers (1967) has alluded to such a dimension when he concludes that what is most personal in the counselling relationship is, almost paradoxically, most universal.

Developing this notion of the transpersonal further, Jung (1978) argued for the existence of a 'collective unconscious' – a domain that contains all human experience, both past and present, to which we all have access. Supporting arguments for the existence of this collective unconscious include the fact of what Jung called synchronicity or meaningful coincidence. We may, for example, be thinking of someone and they phone us or we are about to say something and the person we are with says exactly the same thing. These are examples of synchronous events. The appearance of symbols in dreams is also offered as evidence for the collective unconscious: Jung maintained that certain types of symbols (crosses and circles, for example) occur through the ages in all parts of the world and in many contexts and cultures. Further, these symbols often appear in our dreams and Jung argues that such appearances were made possible through our tapping the collective unconscious. Jung did not offer the concept dogmatically but suggested that it may be a useful one in order to try to make sense of those aspects of self that seem to be shared by all persons.

The self-as-defined-by-others

The self-as-defined-by-others refers to the way in which others see us. This is a particularly complicated issue in that how others see us will depend upon so many variables. Their perception of us will be coloured by at least the following factors – their relationship to us, their previous experiences of people who are like us and different to us, how they think we view them, their views on sexuality, race and roles, their own view of themselves. The matter is further complicated by the fact that other people's perception of us is, presumably, not static. It changes according to the aforementioned variables and in accordance with our relationship with them. This issue of the self-as-defined-by-others is of particular importance in counselling. The client's view of us will go through many phases as the relationship unfolds and this view will be coloured by their changing relationship with themselves. The client's view of the counsellor at any given time in the relationship may serve as a useful barometer for measuring the nature and depth of the relationship. At times, the view of the counsellor will be unequivocally positive; at others it will be far less so. All of these changes reflect, to a greater or lesser degree the amount of dependence and independence that the client is maintaining at that particular time. This changing concept of the counsellor in the eyes of the client has been called **transference** and this is explored further in Chapter 9.

These, then, are some of the many facets that go to make up a sense of self. Another way of making sense of the concept of self is to view it in terms of different types of knowledge.

THE SELF DEFINED THROUGH TYPES OF KNOWLEDGE

Three types of knowledge that go to make up an individual may be described: propositional knowledge, practical knowledge and experiential knowledge (Heron, 1981b). Whilst each of these types is different, each is interrelated with the other. Thus, whilst propositional knowledge may be considered as qualitatively different to, say, practical knowledge, it is possible and probably better, to use propositional knowledge in the application of practical knowledge.

Propositional knowledge

Propositional knowledge is knowledge that is contained in theories or models. It may be described as textbook knowledge and is synonymous with Ryle's (1949) concept of 'knowing that', which was developed further in an educational context by Pring (1976). Thus, a person may build up a considerable bank of facts, theories or ideas about a subject, person or thing, without necessarily having any direct experience of that subject, person or thing. A person, may, for example, develop a considerable propositional knowledge about, say, midwifery, without ever necessarily having been anywhere near a woman who is having a baby! Presumably, it would be more useful to combine that knowledge with some practical experience, but this does not necessarily have to be the case. This, then, is the domain of propositional knowledge. Obviously it is possible to have propositional knowledge about a great number of subject areas ranging from mathematics to literature or from counselling to social work. Any information contained in books (including this one!) must necessarily be of the propositional sort.

Practical knowledge

Practical knowledge is knowledge that is developed through the acquisition of skills. Thus, driving a car or giving an injection demonstrates practical knowledge, though equally, so does the use of counselling skills that involve the use of specific verbal and non-verbal behaviours and intentional use of counselling interventions as described on p. 17. Practical knowledge is synonymous with Ryle's (1949) concept of 'knowing how', which was developed further in an educational context by Pring (1976). Usually more than a mere

47

knack, practical knowledge is the substance of a smooth performance of a practical or interpersonal skill. A considerable amount of a health professional's time is taken up with the demonstration of practical knowledge – often, but not always, of the interpersonal sort.

Traditionally, most educational programmes in schools and colleges have concerned themselves primarily with both propositional and practical knowledge, particularly the former. Thus the propositional knowledge aspect of a person is the aspect that is often held in highest regard. Practical knowledge, although respected, is usually seen as slightly less important than the propositional sort. In this way, the self can become highly developed in one sense – the propositional knowledge aspect – at the expense of being skilled in a practical sense.

Experiential knowledge

The domain of experiential knowledge is knowledge gained through direct encounter with a subject, person or thing. It is the subjective and affective nature of that encounter that contributes to this sort of knowledge. Experiential knowledge is knowledge through relationship. Such knowledge is synonymous with Rogers' (1983) description of experiential learning and with Polanyi's concept of 'personal' knowledge and 'tacit' knowledge (Polanyi, 1958). If we reflect for a moment, we may discover that most of the things that are really important to us belong in this domain. If, for example, we consider our personal relationships with other people, we discover that what we like or love about them cannot be reduced to a series of propositional statements and yet the feelings we have for them are vital and part of what is most important in our lives. Most encounters with others contain the possible seeds of experiential knowledge. It is only when we are so detached from other people that we treat them as objects that no experiential learning can occur.

Not that all experiential knowledge is tied exclusively to relationships with other people. For example, I had considerable propositional knowledge about America before I went there. When I went there, all that propositional knowledge was changed considerably. What I had known was changed by my direct experience of the country. I had developed experiential knowledge of the place. Experiential knowledge is not of the same type or order as propositional or practical knowledge. It is, nevertheless, important knowledge, in that it affects everything else we think about or do.

Experiential knowledge is necessarily personal and idiosyncratic. Indeed, as Rogers (1985) points out, it may be difficult to convey to another person in words. Words tend to be loaded with personal (often experiential) meanings and thus to understand each other we need to understand the nature of the way in which the people with whom we converse use words. It is arguable, however, that such experiential knowledge is sometimes conveyed to others through gesture, eye contact, tone of voice, inflection and all the other nonverbal and paralinguistic aspects of communication (Argyle, 1975). Indeed, it may be experiential knowledge that is passed on when two people (for example a counsellor and her client) become very involved with each other in a conversation, a learning encounter or counselling. Counselling, then, may be concerned very much with the discussion of experiential knowledge: certainly it is more about this domain than it is about the domains of propositional or practical knowledge.

These three domains of knowledge are important aspects of a sense of self. What we know in these three domains is what we are. Thus, a balanced sense of self within this framework is achieved by a balance between our theoretical knowledge, what we can do with it in terms of practical and interpersonal skill and what we have in terms of personal experience. All three domains grow and increase throughout the life cycle, though they are not always equally recognized. As we have seen, propositional knowledge tends to take precedence over the other two and, in academic terms, experiential knowledge often counts for very little.

From the points of view of counselling and of self-awareness, it may be useful to keep all three aspects in balance. The skilled counsellor, then, is one who combines theoretical knowledge about counselling with well-developed interpersonal competence and considerable life experience.

THE CONCEPT OF PERSONHOOD

Yet another way of considering the self is via the notion of **personhood**: what it means to be a person. If we can identify those basic criteria that distinguish persons from all other sorts of things, we may be clearer about what it means to talk of the self. Bannister and Fransella offer a list of criteria for personhood that may be helpful in clarifying such a notion:

It is argued you consider yourself a person in that:

1. You entertain a notion of your own separateness from others; you rely on the privacy of your own consciousness;
2. You entertain a notion of the integrality or completeness of your experience, so that you believe all parts of it are relatable because you are the experiencer;
3. You entertain a notion of your own continuity over time; you possess your own biography and live in relation to it;
4. You entertain a notion of the causality of your actions: you have purposes, you intend, you accept a partial responsibility for the effects of what you do;
5. You entertain a notion of other persons by analogy with yourself; you assume a comparability of subjective experience.

(Bannister and Fransella, 1986)

Such a notion of personhood can do much to clarify both what it means to entertain a notion of self and may also serve as a framework for understanding the personal factors that we are addressing in the process of counselling. For if we accept Bannister and Fransella's idea of personhood, then we necessarily accept that idea as applying to the person who is in front of us in the counselling relationship. The notion of personhood addresses the concepts of separateness from others, completeness of human experience, personal biography, at least partial responsibility for actions and appreciation of other persons as being similar to ourselves. All of these concepts are addressed when one person sets out to counsel another.

AN INTEGRATED MODEL OF THE SELF

What is needed now is a model that brings together the notions of self so far described. Figure 3.1 offers a fairly comprehensive model of the self through which to understand the idea of self-awareness. It incorporates Jung's work on the four functions of the mind: thinking, feeling, sensing and intuiting (Jung, 1978) and also an adaptation of Laing's (1959) concept of an inner and outer self. The outer, public aspect of the self is what others see of us and is compatible with the notion of the self-as-defined-by-others, described on p. 46. The inner, private aspect is what goes on in our heads and bodies. In one sense, the outer experience is what other people are most

Figure 3.1 An integrated model of the self.

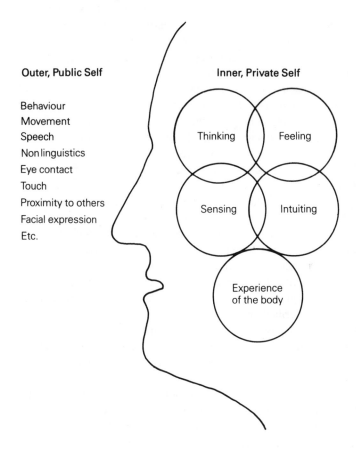

familiar with. We communicate the inner experience through the outer. Our thoughts, feelings and experiences are all communicated through this outer experience of behaviour. Of what does it consist?

The outer experience of the self

At its most simple, behaviour consists of body movements, the crossing of arms and legs, walking, running and so forth. At a more subtle level, however, the issue becomes more complicated. There are a whole variety of more subtle behaviours that convey the inner sense of self through the outer. First, there is speech. What we say

– the words, phrases, metaphors, expressions we use are a potent means by which we convey feelings, thoughts and experiences to others. How we come to choose these particular words, phrases and expressions, however, depends upon a wide range of variables including our past experiences, our education, our cultural inheritance, our knowledge of the language, our attitudes, our belief systems, our social position and the company we are in. Alongside those words and phrases are a whole range of nonlinguistic aspects of speech, including timing, pitch, pacing, silences and so on. The use of such nonlinguistic aspects of communication are subtle ways of communicating aspects of our inner selves to others.

When we talk to other people, we usually look at them. Heron (1970) notes that there can be a wide variety in the intensity, amount and quality of eye contact. Our emotional status and our relationship with the person with whom we are speaking tend to govern the amount of eye contact we allow ourselves to make with them and the amount we expect in return. In the context of counselling, it is important to remain sensitive to aspects of eye contact and to consciously monitor the amount we use in relation to the client. Such monitoring of eye contact is in line with the notion of conscious use of the self, described on p. 52.

The amount of physical contact or touch that we have with others is also a potent means of conveying our inner experience to others. Typically, we touch more those people to whom we are close: members of the family, people we love and very close friends. Some people, it would seem, are 'high touchers' and others 'low touchers'. There are also cultural factors governing the use of touch between people of different races, between the sexes and between people of different relative status. Again, in the context of counselling we need to be careful that our use of touch is unambiguous, acceptable to the client and never viewed by that person as an intrusion. If we are a high toucher, for example, we cannot assume that all of our clients are also high touchers!

When we relate to others, the fact of verbally communicating with them means that we necessarily are near them. How we sit or stand in relation to others is determined, again, by a number of factors, including the level of intimacy we have with them, our relationship with them, certain cultural factors, personal preferences for closeness or lack of it and whether or not we occupy a dominant or subordinate position *vis-à-vis* the other person (Brown, 1986). In the counselling relationship it is easy for the counsellor not to realize that she is occupying a dominant position in that relationship by the very nature of being the counsellor! As a result, the temptation is sometimes to sit closer to the client than is comfortable for him. An easy, practical solution to this is to allow the client to draw up the chair and thus to define the personal space between counsellor and client.

Another indicator of our inner experience is our facial expression. Raised eyebrows, grins and sneers can do much to convey to others our internal status. An important concept, here, is that of **congruence** in communication. Bandler and Grinder (1975) identify three aspects of congruence. A person is said to be congruent when:

1. what they say, matches
2. how they say it and
3. both are matched by the appropriate facial expression

If one or more of these factors mismatch, then communication is likely to be unclear. Sometimes these mismatches are caused by internal conflicts or by our not saying what we really mean. In terms of counselling, it is important that we learn to be congruent in our dealings with others. We must be seen to mean what we say: just saying it is not sufficient! Such congruence needs careful attention and a considerable amount of self-awareness. It is surprising how easily ambiguous thoughts 'leak out' through our facial expressions! External congruence in terms of words, tone of voice and facial expression also calls for internal congruence in terms of our being clear about what we think and feel about what we are saying. It is rare that we can completely disguise our internal thoughts and feelings and anyway, if we are to be genuine in our counselling, it is important that we be clear, honest and unambiguous.

These, then, are aspects of the outer self – that part of ourselves that others see and through which we communicate our inner experience. Not that such outer, visible behaviour is read by others entirely accurately. When other people perceive us, they do so through their own particular frame of reference and tend to interpret what they see in terms of that frame. No-one views another objectively. Everyone's perception of others is more-or-less coloured by their own history and experience. All the more reason, then, as counsellors to ensure that our external behaviour is as clear and as genuine as it can be. It *will* be misread by the client at times, but less so if our initial intentions are clear.

The inner experience of the self

The inner, private experience of the self may be divided into (a) aspects of mental function according to Jung's typography: thinking, feeling, sensing and intuiting and (b) the experience of the body. As we have already noted, this division will necessarily be artificial as both mental and physical events are inextricably linked. As Searle (1983) acknowledges, a mental event is also a physical one. Physical status also affects mental and psychological performance and a person's self-concept. It is interesting to note the growing interest in healing this apparent split between the mind and the body. Increasingly, the move is towards a holistic approach in health care that emphasizes the interrelatedness between mind, body and (sometimes) spirit. Any concept of self must take into account the mind and body as a totality.

Thinking

Thinking refers to all the aspects of our mental processes, both logical and illogical. If we reflect on thinking we will realize that it is not a linear process. We do not think in sentences or even in logical sequences of phrases. The whole process is much more haphazard than that and has much in common with the technique known as **free association**, used in psychoanalysis. Free association asks of the client that he repeats whatever comes into his mind. The result is usually a string of not obviously related statements, ideas and expressions of feelings. Such, perhaps, is the nature of thinking.

Nor can we be sure that our thinking is accurate or realistic. As we noted in the last chapter, Kelly (1955) argued that we are continually creating hypotheses about how the world is and then testing those hypotheses in the light of our experience. In this sense, then, thinking may be concerned with the creation of a number of theories about the world. Guy Claxton suggests an important pair of principles on this issue. He argues that:

(a) What I do depends on what my theory tells me about the world, not on how the world really is. . . and
(b) What happens next depends on how the world really is, not how I believe it to be.

(Claxton, 1984)

Thus, if our theory about how the world is is very distorted, there will be a sense of jarring as we progress through it. If our theory about the world is grounded in some sort of reality, then our perception of the world and our place in it will be that much more congruent. This, again, has implications for counselling. The thing that causes many people discomfort in their lives is, arguably, that they hold in their heads a particular view or set of beliefs about the world that does not match reality. This, in turn, may lead to the sort of thinking that is prefaced by expressions such as 'if only. . ', 'things would be much easier if. . .', 'I know there's no point in thinking like this, but. . .'. All such thoughts tend to lead to a distorted picture of what is actually happening in a person's life. Part of the process of counselling may be to enable people to identify these false perceptions and to clarify them. This is not to argue that there is one true way of looking at the world but to note that people need to be happy for themselves that what goes on in their heads bears a reasonable resemblance to how things actually are in the world.

So, too, must the counsellor work at the process of clarifying her thoughts in line with what she actually perceives about the world. This can be done in a variety of ways – through talking things through with a colleague or a friend, through reading and continuing education and through introspection – the process of looking inward and exploring what the poet Gerard Manley Hopkins called the 'inscape' (Hopkins, 1953).

Feeling

Feeling refers to the emotional aspects of the person: joy, love, anger, disappointment and so forth. Heron (1977a) argues that in our present society we have learned to hold onto or to repress many of our feelings because the cultural norm dictates that we do not overtly express them – particularly the stronger expressions of anger, tears, fear and embarrassment. He argues, also, that such repression leads to the person carrying round with them a great deal of unexpressed feeling that acts as a block to rational thinking, creativity and general enjoyment of life.

Counselling is frequently concerned with allowing people to express such pent-up emotions and there seems to be a direct link between the degree to which a counsellor can freely and appropriately express her own emotions and the degree to which she can **allow** the client to express his. It seems as though if we block off a lot of our own stronger feelings, when we are faced with another person who wants to express feelings we feel reticent about allowing them to do so. Very often this is because the other person's emotion stirs up memories of our own feelings. As we have hung on to them for so long, a mechanism seems to come into play that encourages us to disallow that expression in others and thus allows us to carry on holding on to our own.

A simple experiment may serve to demonstrate the degree to which we carry around bottled-up emotion. Next time you feel moved to tears by something that you see on television, switch off the set and allow yourself to cry. Then listen inwardly to what you are crying about. The chances are that it will be something to do with your own personal history rather than being related directly to what you saw on the screen.

The health professional who is concerned with counselling many people who wish to express pent-up feelings should seriously consider exploring their own emotional status. This can be done through the medium of counselling supervision, in which the counsellor meets regularly with another trained counsellor and talks through and explores their work load. It can also be achieved through the process known as co-counselling, which is described in Chapter 9. It can also help to join a peer-support group (Ernst and Goodison, 1981) in which feelings can be explored in a safe and supportive atmosphere. Such support groups can be instituted and facilitated by a number of like-thinking colleagues and can do much to relieve the pressure of working with the emotionally stressed. Without such support, the health professional can easily slip into a position where she can no longer help the person who wants to express feelings because her own emotional needs are not catered for. The net result, as we noted earlier, can be burnout – a feeling of profound physical and emotional exhaustion caused by job-related stress. Self-awareness, then, must concern itself not only with the thinking side of the person but also with the feelings or emotional side.

Sensing

Sensing refers to inputs through the five special senses: touch, taste, smell, hearing, sight and also to proprioceptive and kinaesthetic sense. Proprioception refers to our ability to know the position of our bodies and thus to know where we are in space. We may note, for instance, that we do not have to think whether or not we are sitting down or standing up: we know that – through our propriocep-tive sense, through bundles of nerve fibres that constantly feed the information back to our brains. Kinaesthetic sense refers to our sense of body movement. Again, this is a sense that we do not normally have to think about – we just move!

Much of the time, we are not aware of the potential stimulation that exists for our senses: we filter out many of the stimuli. A short experiment will illustrate how this filtering process works. Stop reading this book for a moment and pay attention to everything coming in through your senses. What can you hear? What can you see? What can you smell? What can you taste? What can you feel? In recognizing these various inputs through the senses, it becomes apparent just how much is normally not noticed in the course of a day. Now, for much of the time, such filtering out is useful in that it allows us to concentrate on a particular task in hand. In terms of counselling, however, it is vital that we learn to develop an acute awareness of the inputs coming in through the senses, particularly those of hearing and of sight. When counselling, we are not only hearing what the client is saying but also paying attention to how they say it – their tone of voice, their inflection, the volume of their voice and so on. Further, we need to pay attention also to the client's appearance in terms of how they are dressed, how they sit and how they use nonverbal communication: eye contact, body movement, touch, proximity to the counsellor and so forth. Without an awareness of these points of communication, we stand to lose a lot of important information that can help to guide us in deciding how best to intervene in the counselling relationship.

Fortunately, the process of developing such awareness is, in one sense, easy – we just have to do it! If an amount of time is set aside each day just to notice what is going on around us, we can quickly learn to extend this period until we are much more acutely aware of sensory input. Such noticing can become a way of life. The process of noticing is often blocked, however, by internal distractions – recurrent thoughts and worries. Clearly, it is less easy to pay such close attention to what is going on around us when our lives are particularly stressful and we are preoccupied for much of the time with some sort of 'internal dialogue'. Certainly we cannot be effective counsellors unless we can give almost total attention to the client and therefore, at times of personal emotional stress the health professional is likely to function less well in the capacity of counsellor. This, perhaps, is another reason why the person who regularly acts in a counselling role should seriously consider peer support of some sort. Such support is not only useful in talking through difficult issues in counselling, but it may also serve as a means of the counsellor working through some of their own problems in living.

Intuiting

The intuitive aspect of the person is perhaps the most undervalued. Intuiting refers to knowledge and insight that arrives independently of the senses. Ornstein (1975), in a study of the two sides of the brain, comes to the conclusion that the intuitive function is associated with the right side of the brain, whilst the more cognitive process is associated with the left. If Ornstein is right, the implication is that if the intuitive aspect is developed further, then both sides of the brain will function optimally. Certainly Ornstein sees the two processes as complimentary and argues, with Jung, that the intuitive side of the person should be developed alongside the more cognitive aspect. Western culture tends to be dominated by the left-brain approach to education and development – certainly rationality is usually viewed as more important than intuition. Ornstein places intuition beyond mere intellectual understanding in terms of importance and suggests the use of metaphors, allegories, music and Sufi fables as the means by which intuition can be developed.

It may be the case that the intuitive aspect of the person is neglected through fear that it may not be trusted. It is probably true that most of us have intended to act at some time from an intuitive feeling but have held back at the last minute because we could not be sure that our intuition was right. On the other hand, many aspects of the counselling process demand an intuitive approach. In order to empathize with another person, we are required to grasp intuitively what it is to be like them. Certainly, very sensitive issues require an intuitive approach – mere logic or rationality is somehow not enough. Carl Rogers noted that whenever he felt a hunch about something that was happening in the counselling relationship, it invariably helped if he verbalized it (Rogers, 1967), although he acknowledged, too, that he often also doubted his own intuitive ability and took the rational approach, only to find out later that his hunch had been accurate! Using intuition consciously and openly takes courage, but used alongside more rational approaches it can enhance the counselling relationship in a way that logic never can.

These four aspects of the internal part of the person – thinking, feeling, sensing and intuiting need to be developed in combination. Jung argued that many people rely heavily on a one sided approach – particularly the thinking/sensing approach. Such people, he argued, prefer rational argument, backed up by evidence through the senses of a fairly concrete nature. In other words, such people dismissed what they could not directly see, hear, taste, smell or touch or which could not be rationally argued about. Such a position, whilst clearly safe, arguably dismisses some of the more subtle and even metaphysical aspects of life. Certainly it tends to denigrate emotional experience and, presumably, dismisses intuition on the grounds of its not being rational! In terms of the counselling relationship, it would seem valuable to develop all four aspects of the self for it is those four aspects that the client very often has problems with. Life problems are not always of the rational, thinking sort. Nor are they concerned only with what can be directly sensed. Many problems in living are directly related to emotions, feelings and sometimes 'un-nameable' problems – problems concerned with the intuitive domain. Herman Hesse sums up the problems of these sorts of issues, our tendency to ignore the feeling and intuitive domains and our temptation to seek too readily clarification through rationality:

> ... each of us paints and misrepresents every day and every hour the jungle of mysteries, transforming it into a pretty garden or a flat, neatly drawn map, the moralist with the help of his maxims, the man of religion with the help of his faith, the engineer with the help of his slide-rule, the painter with the help of his palette, and the poet with the help of his examples and ideals. And each one of us lives completely and content and assured in his pseudo-world and on his map, just so long as he does not feel, through some breach in the dam or some frightful flash of lightning, reality, the monster, the terrifying beauty, the appalling horror, falling upon him, inescapably embracing him and lethally taking him prisoner.
>
> (Hesse, 1979)

The experience of the body

Another aspect of this integrated model of the self is the experience of the body. If, as has been argued, the mind and body are inextricably linked, then any mental activity will manifest itself as some sort of bodily change and vice versa. It is notable, however, how often we divide the two up. Expressions such as 'my mind is OK, it's my body that's the problem' and 'I'm not happy with my body' indicate how easy it is to make this artificial distinction. A moment's reflection, however, will reveal how artificial this distinction really is. In fact, we do not have a mind and body, we are our mind and body. When we speak of the self, we are speaking of both aspects – mind and body.

Coming to notice the sometimes small changes that take place in the mind/body takes time and patience. Stop reading for a moment and notice your own body. What do you notice? Do you have areas of muscle tension – in the shoulders or neck, for example? What parts of the body are you not aware of? Have any bodily sensations changed since you started noticing? What is your breathing like? Fast, slow, deep or shallow? Many of these small changes in the body tempo can help us to locate changes in mood. Often the first symptom of a mood or state of mind is a bodily change. In learning to notice the body, we can learn to make valuable observations about ourselves and thus further develop self-awareness. Such noticing is also of value in the counselling relationship, for a client's emotions are also often expressed in physical terms. A sudden change of breathing rate can indicate rising anxiety, for example. Psychological tension is often expressed in the form of tightened muscles.

Learning to listen to the body in this way can help us more accurately to assess our true feelings about ourselves and others. Wilhelm Reich (1949), a contemporary of Freud and a psychoanalyst who was particularly interested in the mind–body relationship, argued that many of us carry around with us unexpressed emotion that is somehow 'stored' in our musculature. Emotions, then, could become trapped in sets of muscles. He maintained that direct manipulation of those sets of muscles could release the emotion trapped within them. Such therapy applied directly to the body has become known as Reichian bodywork and can be a powerful means of releasing pent-up emotion and gaining self-awareness through a very direct method.

Similiar but different versions of this physical approach to psychological issues may be found in Rolfing (Rolf, 1973), bioenergetics (Lowen, 1967), Feldenkrais (Feldenkrais, 1972) and the Alexander technique (Alexander, 1969). Other examples of the approach to self-awareness through the mind–body include massage, yoga, the martial arts, certain types of meditation, dance and certain sorts of sports and exercise.

All of these methods can enhance self-awareness through attention to changes in the body and thus create insight into psychological states. They can also aid development of awareness of body image.

If we notice people in everyday life, we may observe how many people walk in a lopsided manner or stoop their shoulders and may even have different sorts of expressions on either side of their face! Bodywork methods may help in balancing the person and may lead to a greater sense of physical (and, therefore, psychological) symmetry. It would seem reasonable to argue that it would be strange to concentrate on developing awareness of the mind whilst totally ignoring the body. Similarly, it is perhaps odd to concentrate on physical fitness or balance without paying attention to psychological status. This joint focus also applies to the process of counselling. Effective counselling involves paying attention to both what the client says and what he does. Thus the mind–body is attended to as a totality.

This, then, is an integrated model of the self, focusing on the outer, public expression of self, through our behaviour and an inner, more private aspect of self. Clearly this is only one way of discussing the self and as we noted earlier, the self has many facets, including the self-as-perceived-by-others. The model offered here, however, may allow us to make a start at developing self-awareness as an important tool in the process of skilful counselling. For self-awareness can never be developed purely for its own sake, but as a means of enhancing our caring and helping skills.

SELF-AWARENESS

What is self-awareness? First, the point needs to be made that it is not self-consciousness in the sense of becoming painfully aware of how we imagine other people see us. Sartre (1956) describes this condition well when he says that when we come under the scrutinizing gaze of another person, we perceive ourselves as being turned into objects by that other person. It is as though we become a thing rather than a person. Such a notion of treating people as things and the resultant self-consciousness is a valuable concept in the context of counselling, for it is important that we do not become interested in the problems of the person we are counselling to the extent that they merely become interesting cases. Once we do this, we have made them into things and as a result they may feel distinctly uncared for and uncomfortable.

Self-awareness is the evolving and expanding sense of noticing and taking account of a wide range of aspects of the self. As we explore our psychological and physical make-up we get to know ourselves

61

better. Chapman and Gale (1982) notice a curious paradox about this process. They note that to gain knowledge of something does not normally change that thing. If, for instance, I learn an equation, that equation does not change as a result of my having learnt it. With self-awareness, however, the subject of the learning – the self – changes as more is learnt about it. In this sense, then, the process of developing self-awareness is a continuous process because we are continuously changing. Self-awareness, curiously, may speed up that change.

Two different and complimentary methods of developing self-awareness may be described. One is through the process of introspection or looking inward. The other is through receiving feedback about ourselves from other people. The two used in balance can lead to a reasonable and hopefully accurate picture of the self. One without the other can lead to a curiously skewed sense of self. Thus, introspection on its own can lead to either an unnecessarily harsh judgement of the self or a narcissistic and self-centred view. Relying only on feedback from others can lead us to concentrate only on the external or public aspect of the self. Again, there is no guarantee that another person's assessment of us is any more or any less accurate than our own but it is important to hear it! To be able to hear it undefensively is yet another skill. Often, when other people tell us what they think of us, for good or bad, we react to it. The skill here may be to accept it, in much the same way as it has been suggested that we accept what the client says to us in counselling. If we can free others to tell us easily their impression of us, we are slightly more likely to get an honest view from them on other occasions. If, however, we always react to what they have to say, then it seems likely that they will be less forthcoming on future occasions. This has implications for work in peer-support groups used as vehicles for self-awareness development. Just as we must be prepared to listen fully to the client in counselling, so we must be prepared to listen fully to our peers in such a group.

Figure 3.2 offers a variety of practical methods for developing self-awareness that may be used by the individual working on her own or by groups of peers working together in a group. It is not suggested that it represents an exhaustive list of self-awareness methods, but it can serve as a starting point. In practice, the individual will often identify particular preferences for certain methods of self-awareness development. It is important, however, to occasionally 'freshen the act' and try new methods!

It is important to note that self-awareness development should be

Figure 3.2 Methods of developing self-awareness.

Aspects of self-awareness	Methods of developing self-awareness
1. *Thinking, including:* – stream of consciousness – belief systems – ideas – fantasies etc.	Discussion/conversation Group work Introspection Brainstorming Meditation Writing Use of problem-solving cycle, etc.
2. *Feelings, including:* – anger – fear – grief – embarrassment – joy/happiness – mood swings etc.	Discussion/conversation Group work Introspection Gestalt exercises Meditation Co-counselling Supervision Analysis Cathartic work Sensitivity training Encounter group work Role play, etc.
3. *Sensations, including:* – taste – touch – hearing – smell – sight – etc.	Focusing attention on one or more sensations at a time Group exercises Use of sensory stimulation/deprivation exercises, gestalt exercises Noticing in everyday life, etc.
4. *Sexuality, including:* – orientation (heterosexual/ homosexual/bisexual – expression of sexuality etc.	Discussion/conversation Counselling/co-counselling Values, clarification exercises, etc.

Aspects of self-awareness	Methods of developing self-awareness
5. *Spirituality, including:* – belief systems – life philosophy – awareness of choice – varieties of religious experience – aetheism and agnosticism etc.	Discussion/conversation Group work Meditation Prayer Reading Aesthetic experience (art, music, poetry, etc.) Life-planning, goal-setting
6. *Physical status, including:* – the body systems – health status etc.	Self-examination Medical examination Exercise Sport Martial arts Meditation Massage Bodywork, etc.
7. *Appearance, including:* – dress – personal style – height, weight etc.	Discussion/conversation Self- and peer assessment Self-monitoring Use of video, etc.
8. *Knowledge, including:* – level of propositional knowledge – level of practical knowledge – level of experimental knowledge	Discussion/conversation Group work Examinations/testing/quizzing Study Use of distance-learning packages Enrolment on courses Self- and peer assessment etc.

Aspects of self-awareness	Methods of developing self-awareness
9. *Needs and wants, including:*	
– financial/material	Discussion/conversation
– physical	Group work
– love and belonging	Values-clarification work
– achievement	Assertiveness training
– knowledge	Life-style evaluation
– aesthetic	etc.
– spiritual	
– self-actualization	
etc.	
10. *Other aspects, including:*	
– verbal and non-verbal skills	Discussion/conversation
– values	Counselling/co-counselling
– unknown/undiscovered aspects of	Self-analysis
– of the self	Social-skills training

an enjoyable process! It should neither be too earnest nor too concentrated. A sense of perspective and a sense of humour is essential to the process as is keeping a sense of the 'larger picture' – the social situation in which the individual exists. A political and social awareness is as vital to the development of counselling skills as is a sense of self-awareness.

SELF-AWARENESS AND THE HEALTH PROFESSIONAL

As we have seen, self-awareness underlies almost every aspect of the counselling relationship. In all of the health professions, the fact that the professional forms close and personal relationships with her clients emphasizes this need for understanding of self. When other people are physically, emotionally, socially or spiritually distressed, that distress cannot but affect us in some way. We need, therefore, not only professional knowledge and know-how, related to our particular speciality and an awareness of how our work fits in with the work of others in the caring team, but also personal awareness that can inform our practice in the health field. Such self-awareness can help us to develop an understanding of the basic principles of counselling discussed in the next chapter.

65

4

Basic principles and considerations

In order to function effectively as a counseller, it is necessary to consider some principles that can enhance or detract from the relationship. First, it may be useful to look at what may be considered the ideal counselling relationship. Fiedler, in 1950 asked a wide variety of counsellors what they considered to be the ingredients of an ideal therapeutic relationship. The list that was generated by his research included:

1. an empathic relationship
2. the therapist and patient relate well
3. the therapist sticks closely to the patient's problems
4. the patient feels free to say what he likes
5. an atmosphere of mutual trust and confidence exists
6. rapport is excellent

(Fiedler, 1950)

In 1957, Carl Rogers developed Fiedler's work and identified what he called the six necessary and sufficient conditions for therapeutic change via the counselling relationship. He argued that the following conditions had to exist and continue for a period if counselling was to be effective:

1. two persons are in psychological contact;
2. the first, who we shall term the client, is in a state of incongruence; vulnerable or anxious;
3. the second person, whom we shall term the therapist, is congruent or integrated in the relationship;
4. the therapist experiences unconditional regard for the client;
5. the therapist experiences an empathic understanding of the

client's internal frame of reference and endeavours to communicate this experience to the client;

6. the communication to the client of the therapist's empathic understanding and unconditional positive regard is to a minimal degree achieved.

(Rogers, 1957)

Whether or not Rogers' claim of these conditions being necessary and sufficient is completely accurate in the philosophical sense of those terms need not concern us here. What is particularly useful is that the list identifies certain personal qualities that must exist in the person in order for them to function as an effective counsellor. The particular personal qualities that Rogers discusses frequently in his writing about counselling are unconditional positive regard, empathic understanding, warmth and genuineness (Rogers, 1967). The need for these qualities is also born out by the research conducted by Truax and Carkuff (1967a) and the characteristics of empathy, warmth and genuineness are often referred to as the 'Truax Triad' (Schulman, 1982). To these qualities may be added those of concreteness and immediacy, also suggested by Carkuff (1969). All of these qualities are worth exploring further as they can lay the foundations for effective counselling in any context.

NECESSARY PERSONAL QUALITIES OF THE EFFECTIVE COUNSELLOR

Unconditional positive regard

Rogers' rather clumsy phrase conveys a particularly important predisposition towards the client, by the counsellor. It is also called **prizing** or even just **accepting**. It means that the client is viewed with dignity and valued as a worthwhile and positive human being. The 'unconditional' prefix refers to the idea that such regard is offered without any preconditions. Often in relationships, some sort of reciprocity is demanded: I will like you (or love you) as long as you return that liking or loving. Rogers is asking that the feelings that the counsellor holds for the client should be undemanding and not requiring reciprocation. Also, there is a suggestion of an inherent goodness within the client. This notion of persons as essentially good can be traced back, at least to Rousseau's *Emile* and is possibly philosophically problematic. Arguably, notions such as goodness and badness are social constructions and to argue that a person is born good or bad is fraught. However, as a practical starting point in the counselling relationship, it seems to be a good idea that we assume an inherent, positive and life-asserting characteristic in the client. It seems difficult to argue otherwise. It would be odd, for instance, to engage in the process of counselling with the view that the person was essentially bad, negative and unlikely to grow or develop! Thus, unconditional positive regard offers a baseline from which to start the counselling relationship. In order to further grasp this concept, it may be useful to refer directly to Rogers' definition of the notion:

> I hypothesize that growth and change are more likely to occur the more that the counsellor is experiencing a warm, positive, acceptant attitude towards what *is* the client. It means that he prizes his client, as a person, with the same quality of feeling that a parent feels for his child, prizing him as a person regardless of his particular behaviour at the moment. It means that he cares for his client in a non-possessive way, as a person with potentialities. It involves an open willingness for the client to be whatever feelings are real in him at the moment – hostility or tenderness, rebellion or submissiveness, assurance or self-depreciation. It means a kind of love for the client as he is, providing we understand the word love as equivalent to the theologian's term *agape*, and not in its usual romantic and possessive meanings. What I am describing is a feeling which is not paternalistic, nor sentimental, nor superficially social and agreeable. It respects the other person as a separate individual and does not possess him. It is a kind of liking which has strength, and which is not demanding. We have termed it positive regard.
>
> (Rogers and Stevens, 1967)

Unconditional positive regard, then, involves a deep and positive feeling for the other person, perhaps equivalent in the health professions to what Alistair Campbell has called 'moderated love' (Campbell, 1984). He talks of 'lovers and professors', suggesting that certain professionals profess to love, thus claiming both the ability to be professional and to express altruistic love or disinterested love for others. The suggestion is also that the health professional has a positive and warm confidence in her own skills and abilities in the counselling relationship. Halmos sums this up when he writes:

'You are worthwhile!' and 'I am not put off by your illness!' This moral stance of not admitting defeat is possible for those who have faith or a kind of stubborn confidence in the rightness of what they are doing.

(Halmos, 1965)

For Halmos, the counselling relationship is something of an act of faith. There can be no guarantee that the counselling offered will be effective but the counsellor enters the relationship with the belief that it will be. It is this positive outlook in the counsellor and this positive belief in the ability of the client to change for the better that is summarized in Rogers' notion of unconditional positive regard (Rogers and Stevens, 1967). Such an outlook is also supported by Egan who, in his 'portrait of a helper' says:

They respect their clients and express this respect by being available to them, working with them, not judging them, trusting the constructive forces found in them, and ultimately placing the expectation on them that they will do whatever is necessary to handle their problems in living more effectively.

(Egan, 1982)

Empathic understanding

Empathy is the ability to enter the perceptual world of the other person: to see the world as they see it. It also suggests an ability to convey this identification of feelings to the other person. Kalisch (1971) defines empathy as 'the ability to perceive accurately the feelings of another person and to communicate this understanding to him'. Whilst Mayeroff (1972), in a classic book on caring, describes empathic understanding from this point of view of caring for another person:

To care for another person I must be able to understand him and his world as if I were inside it. I must be able to see, as it were, with his eyes what his world is like to him and how he sees himself. Instead of merely looking at him in a detached way from outside, as if he were a specimen I must be able to be *with* him in his world, 'going' into his world in order to sense from 'inside' what life is like for him, what he is striving to be, and what he requires to grow.

(Mayeroff, 1972)

Empathy is clearly different to sympathy. Sympathy suggests feeling sorry for the other person or, perhaps, identifying with how they feel. If I sympathize, I imagine myself as being in the other person's position and imagine how I would feel. If I empathize, however, I try to imagine how it is to be the other person – feeling sorry for him does not really come into the issue.

As with unconditional positive regard, the process of developing empathy involves something of an act of faith. When we empathize with another person, we cannot know what the outcome of that empathizing will be. If we pre-empt the outcome of our empathizing, we are already not empathizing – we are thinking of solutions and of ways of influencing the client towards a particular goal that we have in mind. The process of empathizing involves entering into the perceptual world of the other person without necessarily knowing where that process will lead to. Martin Buber the Hassidic philosopher, mystic and writer on psychotherapy, summed up well this mixture of willingness to explore the world of the other without presupposing the outcome, when he wrote:

A man lost his way in a great forest. After awhile another lost his way and chanced on the first. Without knowing what had happened to him, he asked the way out of the woods.
'I don't know', said the first. 'But I can point out the ways that lead further into the thicket, and after that let us try to find the way together'.

(Buber, 1948)

The process of developing empathic understanding is the process of exploring the client's world, with the client neither judging nor suggesting. It can be achieved best through the process of careful attending and listening to the other person and, perhaps, by use of the skills known as **reflection** discussed in a later chapter of this book (p. 122). Essentially, though, it is also a way of being, a disposition towards the client, a willingness to explore and intuitively allow the other person to express themselves fully. Again, as with unconditional positive regard and with all aspects of the client-centred approach to counselling, the empathic approach is under-pinned by the idea that it is the client in the end who will find his own way through and will find his own, idiosyncratic answers to his problems in living. To be empathic is to be a fellow traveller, a friend to the person as they undertake the search. Empathic understanding, then, involves the notion of befriending alluded to in

Chapter 1. Just as a friend can (usually!) accept another friend 'warts and all', so the counsellor, in being empathic, is offering such acceptance.

There are, of course, limitations to the degree to which we can truly empathize. Because we all live in different worlds based on our particular culture, education, physiology, belief systems and so forth, we all view that world slightly differently. Thus, to truly empathize with another person would involve actually becoming that other person! Clearly impossible! We can, however, strive to get as close to the perceptual world of the other by listening and attending and by suspending judgement. We can also learn to forget ourselves temporarily and give ourselves as completely as we can to the other person.

In the following dialogue, a young girl, Rebecca, is talking to her social worker, about the situation at home. The dialogue illustrates something of the nature of developing empathy.

Rebecca: I don't know, I just don't seem to be getting on with people.

Social worker: When you say people?

Rebecca: I mean my parents. They don't have any idea.

Social worker: They don't have any idea about you?

Rebecca: No, they think that I want to stay at school and go to university and everything. Well, I do, in a way. But I wish they wouldn't push me all the time! They think they have to tell me how to do things all the time.

Social worker: It's as if they want to push you in a certain direction and you're not sure whether or not you want to go that way.

Rebecca: That's exactly it! I don't know what I want to do any more! They push me so much that I don't know what I want!

Social worker: And that's upsetting you?

Rebecca: Yeah, a lot... I get upset easily these days and I'm sure it's got a lot to do with what's happening at home.

In this example, the two people become closely involved in the conversation and the social worker, rather than directing the conversation in a particular way, follows the thoughts and feelings that Rebecca expresses. Empathy is developed through this following process and through a willingness to listen to both what is said and what is implied in what is being said. An intuitive ability is just as important in empathy as is technical skill.

Warmth and genuineness

Warmth in the counselling relationship refers to a certain approach-
ability and willingness to be open with the client. Schulman (1982)
notes that the following characteristics are included in the concept of
warmth – equal worth, absence of blame, nondefensiveness and
closeness. Warmth is a frame of mind rather than a skill and perhaps
one developed through being honest with oneself and being prepared
to be open with others. It is also about treating the other person as
an equal human being. Martin Buber (1958) distinguishes between
the I–it relationship and the I–thou (or I–you) relationship. In the I–
it relationship, one person treats the other as an object, a thing. In
the I–thou relationship, there occurs a meeting of persons, despite
any differences there may be in terms of status, background,
lifestyle, belief or value systems. In the I–thou relationship there is
a sense of mutuality, a sense that can be contagious and is of
particular value in the counselling relationship:

In a meaningful friendship, caring is mutual, each cares for the
other; caring becomes contagious. My caring for the other helps
activate his caring for me; and similarly his caring for me helps
activate my caring for him, it 'strengthens' me to care for him.
(Mayeroff, 1972)

What is less clear, however, is the degree to which a counselling
relationship can be a mutual relationship. Rogers (1967) argues that
the counselling relationship can be a mutual relationship but Buber
acknowledges that because it is always the client who seeks out the
counsellor and comes to that counsellor with problems, the relationship is, necessarily, unequal and lacking in mutuality:

He comes for help to you. You don't come for help to him. And
not only this, but you are *able*, more or less to help him. He
can do different things to you, but not help you... You are, of
course, a very important person for him. But not a person whom
he wants to see and to know and is able to. He is floundering
around, he comes to you. He is, may I say, entangled in your
life, in your thoughts, in your being, your communication, and
so on. But he is not interested in you as you. It cannot be.
(Buber, 1966)

Thus warmth must be offered by the counsellor but the feeling cannot necessarily be reciprocated by the client. There is, as well, another problem with the notion of warmth. We each perceive personal qualities in different sorts of ways. One person's warmth is another person's patronage or sentimentality. We cannot guarantee how our presentation of self will be perceived by the other person. In a more general way, however, warmth may be compared to coldness. It is clear that the cold person would not be the ideal person to undertake counselling! Further, our relationships with others tend to be self-monitoring to a degree: we anticipate as we go, the effect we are having on others and modify our presentation of self accordingly. Thus, we soon get to know if our warmth is suffocating the client or is being perceived by him in a negative way. Certainly this ability to constantly monitor ourselves and our relationships is an important part of the process of developing counselling skills.

Genuineness, too, is an important facet of the relationship. We either care for the person in front of us or we do not. We cannot fake professional interest. We must be interested. Now, clearly, some people will interest us more than others. Often, those clients who remind us at some level of our own problems or our own personalities will interest us most of all. This is not so important as our having a genuine interest in the fact that the relationship is happening at all. The strength of interest is not the important issue but the commitment to involvement is.

There may appear to be a conflict between the concept of genuineness and the self-monitoring alluded to above. Self-monitoring may be viewed as artificial or contrived and therefore not genuine. The genuineness discussed here relates to the counsellor's interest in the human relationship that is developing between the two people. Any ways in which that relationship can be enhanced must serve a valuable purpose. It is quite possible to be genuine and yet aware of what is happening: genuine and yet commited to increasing interpersonal competance.

Genuineness starts with self-awareness. This is summed up in Shakespeare's observation:

This above all – to thine own self be true;
And it must follow, as the night the day,
Thou canst not then be false to any man.

(*Hamlet*, act 1, scene 3)

Egan sums up the notion of genuineness in the context of counselling when he identifies the following aspects of it:

You are genuine in your relationship with your clients when you:
- do not overemphasize your professional role and avoid stereotyped role behaviours
- are spontaneous but not uncontrolled or haphazard in your relationships
- remain open and non-defensive even when you feel threatened
- are consistent and avoid discrepancies – between your values and your behaviour, and between your thoughts and your words in interactions with clients – while remaining respectful and reasonably tactful
- are willing to share yourself and your experience with clients if it seems helpful

(Egan, 1986b)

Concreteness

Concreteness refers to the idea that the counsellor should be clear and explicit in her dealings with the client and should help the client to express himself clearly. This is essential if communication between the two parties is to be successful. Concreteness involves helping the client to put into words those things that are only being hinted at in order that both client and counsellor are understanding what the client is perceiving at any given time. The following conversation demonstrates the counsellor attempting to develop this sense of concreteness.

Client: I don't know, I feel sort of disinterested a lot of the time... as if no-one cared much about what was going on.
Counsellor: You seem to be saying two things: you feel disinterested and you feel that no-one cares for you.
Client: They're not interested in what I do.
Counsellor: Other people aren't interested in you?
Client: Yes, that's right. I'm O.K... it's just that other people don't want to know about me;
Counsellor: When you say other people, who do you mean?
Client: You know... my family... my wife especially.

In this way, the counsellor helps the client to clarify what he is saying and enables him to be more specific. Without such clarification it is possible for both parties to be talking to each other without either really understanding the other. Whenever the counsellor senses that she is losing the client it is useful for her to return to this concrete approach.

It is important, too, that the counsellor does not mystify the client by overpowering him with technique or with unasked-for interpretations. This is another sense of the notion of being concrete. The client should at no time feel threatened by the counselling relationship nor feel that the counsellor is 'doing something strange'. Sometimes, the person new to counselling will feel more comfortable hiding behind a mystique and a sense of being a therapist. Such behaviour cuts across the notions of remaining warm and empathic. The counselling relationship should remain clear and unmysterious to the client. Rogers (1967) has used the word transparent to describe this sense of openness and clarity.

Immediacy

When people are distressed by the life situation in which they find themselves when they talk in a counselling relationship, there is a temptation for them to spend a considerable amount of time reminiscing about the past. Somehow, it seems safer to talk of the past rather than face feelings in the here-and-now. One of the tasks of the counsellor is to help the client to identify present thoughts and feelings. In this way, current issues are addressed and problem-solving can relate directly to those present-day issues. This is not to say that the client should never be allowed to talk about the past but to note that the counsellor may function more effectively if they keep a check on the degree to which such reminiscing occurs. In a sense the present is all there is: the past is past and the future has not yet arrived. The client who talks excessively about how things were avoids the reality of the present.

'DON'TS' IN THE COUNSELLING RELATIONSHIP

Having identified some of the qualities and characteristics that go to make up an effective counselling relationship, it is time to turn to some things that do not enhance it. These can be discussed most easily in the form of a list of 'don'ts'. Like any such list, there will be occasions on which any one of these items may be helpful in the counselling relationship: that is an illustration of how such relationships are unique and unpredictable! As a general rule, however, the following issues run contrary to the qualities identified above and are best avoided.

Don't ask 'why' questions

(Example: Why do you feel depressed?)
The word why suggests interrogation, probing and a sense of disapproval. Further, the 'why' question can encourage the client to discuss their feelings in a theoretical way. In other words, when the counsellor asks the client why he is depressed, she is inviting him to offer a theory about why he feels that way. In the following example of dialogue between a community psychiatric nurse and her patient, we see this shift from feelings to theory.

> *Nurse:* Tell me a bit more about how you're feeling at the moment.
> *Patient:* It's difficult to say... I feel depressed, really.
> *Nurse:* Why do you feel like that?
> *Patient:* My mother was depressive... perhaps I take after her...

The 'why' question in this example does nothing to help the patient expand on his expression of feeling but leads him immediately to offer a theoretical explanation of his feelings. 'Why' questions are best avoided altogether in the context of counselling, although a considerable effort may have to be exerted on the part of the new counsellor to drop them from her repertoire! 'Why' questions tend to be very frequent ones in everyday conversation and the temptation to ask them can be very strong. Perhaps, too, they derive from an almost inherent sense of nosiness that most of us feel at some time or another!

Don't use 'shoulds' and 'oughts'

(Example: You realize that what you should do is...)
Moralizing rarely helps. When the counsellor suggests what the other person should do, she forces her own frame of reference, her own value system, on the client. It is difficult to imagine many situations in which a counsellor can really advise another person about what they should do. Possible exceptions to this rule are those

situations in which concrete facts are under discussion. For example, a doctor may suggest that a patient should finish a course of medicine. In counselling, however, the issues under discussion are usually the client's problems in living. The counsellor's value system is rarely of use in helping the client to untangle his life and find a solution to his problem.

Don't blame

(Example: I'm not surprised, you've been very stupid.)
As with the question of 'oughts' and 'shoulds', trying to suggest or apportion blame is not constructive. In a sense, it doesn't matter who is to blame in any particular situation. The point is that a situation has occurred and the client is trying to find ways of dealing with it.

Don't automatically *compare the client's experience with your own experience*

(Example: I know exactly what you mean. . . I'm like that too. . .)
The key word, here, is automatically. Sometimes, shared experience can be helpful to the client. Often, however, it can lead to an exchange of experiences that is neither helpful nor progressive. Luft (1969) uses the descriptor **parallaction** to describe the sorts of parallel conversations that can occur as a result of such comparison. In the following example, two friends are discussing the previous evening.

> I had a good night, last night. Went to the cinema.
> Yes, we went out to a restaurant.
> I hadn't seen a film for months.
> We don't get out for meals very often.
> I saw *Gone With the Wind*. . . it must be 30 years old!
> Have you seen David in the last few weeks?

In the conversation, neither person is really listening to the other. Each wants to talk about himself and neither is prepared to hear the other. Clearly, such an exaggerated situation is unlikely to occur in counselling, but it is surprising how such comparisons of experience can lead down blind alleys. An example of how this can occur is as follows. The conversation is between a social worker and her client:

Client: I get very anxious, sometimes. . . especially when I've got exams coming up.

Social worker: I suppose everybody does. . . I know I do. . .

Client: I get to think that I won't make it. . . that I'm not good enough.

Social worker: I know what you mean. I thought I wouldn't get my social-work exams. . . I got really upset.

The counselling relationship belongs to the client: it is his time to explore his problems. If the counsellor constantly compares her own experience with that of the client, she is taking away some of that time from the client. More importantly, perhaps, she is saying to the client, 'Your problems are my problems.' And yet, it is the client who is coming to see the counsellor and not vice versa! It is likely that if the counsellor expresses such similarity of experience to the client, the latter will resent it, for how can it be that both have similar problems and yet one has to sort out the other to help solve those problems? Such a contradiction can confuse and irritate the client and spoil the counselling relationship.

Don't invalidate the client's feelings

(Example: Of course you're not angry/depressed/in love. . . you just think you are. . .)

This sort of judgement is a curious one. It suggests a number of possibilities: (a) the client is not telling the truth, (b) the client doesn't use words appropriately (presumably in accordance with the counsellor's definitions!) or (c) the counsellor is better able to judge the client's feelings than the client himself. Yet such interventions are by no means rare. Rarely are they therapeutic. A more appropriate approach may be to explore the expressed feeling in order to understand more fully the way in which the client is using words to describe feelings.

These, then, are some 'don'ts'. They are approaches to counselling interventions that are best avoided in that they are either heavily prescriptive, judgemental or inappropriate. As we have noted, there will be times when each is appropriate with this client at this point in time – particularly, perhaps, as the counselling relationship develops and both counsellor and client get to know each other better.

QUESTIONS TO CONSIDER PRIOR TO COUNSELLING

QUESTIONS TO CONSIDER PRIOR TO COUNSELLING

Prior to commencing counselling, there are some questions that may usefully be considered in order to establish whether or not I am the appropriate person to counsel this person at this time.

Am I the appropriate person to counsel?

Sometimes we are too close to the person who comes to us for counselling. The concept of **therapeutic distance** is useful here. If we are emotionally too involved with the other person, we are probably too close to them to be able to stand back from them and assess their situation with reasonable objectivity. On the other hand, it is possible to stand too far back and be so detached from the other person that we are unable to appreciate their problems with any sensitivity at all. There would appear to be an optimum position in which to stand in relation to the client so that we are both disinterested and involved. Examples of people with whom we may be too involved include members of our family and close friends. Examples of people from whom we may be too distanced include (paradoxically) those people who present us with a number of problems that are very similar to our own and those people who are so different to us that we fail basically to even empathize with them.

Have I the time to counsel?

Counselling takes time. It is tempting to think that, at the outset we may easily be able to afford the time we offer the client. This seems to be no problem when the client is initially depressed and it does not seem unreasonable to offer time. Once the client has begun to unravel some of his problems, the time factor becomes more pressing and it is remarkably easy to find that we are no longer sure that we have the time! It is important that we decide at the outset of the counselling relationship that we will be able to apportion adequate time for the other person. If we cannot, we should consider referring him to someone else.

On the other hand, there is much to be said for structuring the amount of time spent in counselling. It is useful to lay down clear time parameters as to the start and finish of the counselling session. It is often true that real client-disclosure occurs towards the end of a counselling session – the important things are said last. If the client has no idea of when the session will end, he will clearly be unable to make these late and important disclosures. This issue of time will be discussed further in the next chapter.

Have I the client's permission to counsel?

It would seem to be a curious notion that counselling can ever take place against the client's will. In a sense, all counselling is voluntary: no-one can be forced to disclose things that they are not ready or willing to disclose. On the other hand, it is easy to pressurize people into thinking that they should be counselled! When this happens, it is arguable that the counselling relationship is no longer a voluntary one: subtle coercion has taken place, it would seem better that it is always the client who seeks out the counsellor and never the counsellor who seeks out the client!

The term permission as it is used here, is nearly always tacit permission: the fact that the client comes to the counsellor at all suggests that he gives permission for counselling to take place. Even when this initial, tacit contract has been established, however, it is important that the counsellor does not become intrusive and attempt to force disclosure where it is not freely offered. It is tempting, at times, for us to believe that disclosure will 'do the other person good'. This is an interesting value judgement but one that may say more about the counsellor's needs than those of the client!

Where will the counselling take place?

In an ideal world, counselling takes place on neutral territory: neither in the client's home nor in the office of the counsellor. Ideally, too, it is conducted in a room that is free from distractions, including other people who may knock on the door, telephones that may ring and surroundings that are so overstimulating that they distract the client's or counsellor's attention away from the task in hand. In practice, however, the environment is usually far removed from meeting these ideal criteria. Very often, counselling takes place wherever it occurs. Few people who work in the health professions can engineer the situation to such a degree that they can set up a particularly appropriate environment.

Having said that, there are environmental factors that may be borne in mind in almost all counselling settings. First, the chairs that both people sit in can be of the same height. This helps to create a certain equality in the relationship. If the counsellor sits at a higher or lower level than the client, it will be difficult for the relationship to develop. When the counsellor is sitting on a higher chair than the client, it puts her in a dominant position. When she is sitting on a lower chair, the relationship is such that the client is placed in a dominant position and may find this counterproductive to the telling of his story and to disclosing himself to the counsellor.

A further consideration is a seemingly odd one. It refers to where the counsellor and client sit in relation to the nearest window! It is difficult if either person sits with the window behind them (unless the lights are on!). If the counsellor sits with her back to the window, she will appear as a rather shadowy form because the client will be unable to see her properly. If the client sits in that position, the counsellor will not be able to see him properly and may miss vital aspects of nonverbal communication that can do much to convey particular thoughts and feelings. More suitable positions are well away from windows or ones in which both counsellor and client sit with the window to one side of them.

These are some important practical considerations that the health professional needs to consider prior to setting out as a counsellor. All of these things need to be borne in mind before the specific skills of counselling are considered. Before such skills are discussed in detail, it may be useful to consider some basic principles of counselling that arise out of the literature and out of the discussion raised so far. These may be enumerated as follows:

1. The client knows what is best for him;
2. Interpretation by the counsellor is likely to be inaccurate and is best avoided;
3. Advice is rarely helpful;
4. The client occupies a different personal world from that of the counsellor and vice versa;
5. Listening is the basis of the counselling relationship;
6. Counselling techniques should not be overused; however,
7. Counselling can be learned.

BASIC PRINCIPLES OF COUNSELLING

The client knows what is best for him

We all perceive the world differently as we have all had different personal histories that colour our views. Throughout our lives we develop a variety of coping strategies and ways of managing that we use when beset by personal problems. Central to client-centred counselling, particularly, is the notion that, given the space and time, we are the best arbiters of what is and what is not right for us. We can listen to other people but in the end we, as individuals, have to decide upon our own courses of action.

Belief in the essential ability of all persons to make worthwhile decisions for themselves arises from the philosophical tradition known as existentialism (Mcquarrie, 1973; Pakta, 1972). Existentialists argue, amongst other things, that we are born free and that we 'create' ourselves as we go through life. For the existentialist, nothing is predetermined: there is no blueprint for how any given person's life will turn out. Responsibility and choice lie squarely with the individual: we choose what we will become. Sartre sums up this position when he argues that:

> Man first of all exists, encounters himself and surges up in the world and defines himself afterwards. If man, as the existentialists see him, is not definable, it is because to begin with he is nothing. He will not be anything until later and then he will be what he makes of himself.
>
> (Sartre, 1973)

No-one is free in all respects. We are born into a particular society, culture, family and body. On the other hand, our psychological make-up is much more fluid and arguably not predetermined. We are free to think and feel. One of the aims of the counselling relationship is to enable the client to realize this freedom to think and feel and, therefore, to act.

Once a person has to some extent recognized this freedom, he begins to realize that he can change his life. This is a central issue in the humanistic approach to counselling: that people can change (Shaffer, 1978). They do not have to be weighed down by the past or by their conditioning: they are more-or-less free to choose their own future. And no-one can choose that future for them. Hence the overriding principle that the client knows what is best for them.

Interpretation by the counsellor is likely to be inaccurate and is best avoided

To interpret, in this sense, is to offer the client an explanation of his thinking, feeling or action. Interpretations are useful in that they can help us to clarify and offer a framework on which the client may make future decisions. However, they are best left to the client to make.

As we have seen, we all live in different perceptual worlds. Because of this, another person's interpretation of my thinking, feeling or action will be based on that person's experience, not mine. That interpretation is, therefore, more pertinent to the person offering it than it is to me, coloured as it is bound to be by the perceptions of the other person. Such colouring is usually more of a hindrance than a help. Often, too, interpretations are laced with moral injunctions – oughts and shoulds. Thus, an interpretation can quickly degenerate into moralistic advice that may lead to the client feeling guilty or rejecting the advice because it does not fit in with his own belief or value system.

Advice is rarely helpful

Attempts to help 'put people's lives right' is fraught with pitfalls. Advice is rarely directly asked for and rarely appropriate. If it is taken, the client tends to assume that 'That's the course of action I would have taken anyway', or he becomes dependent on the counsellor. The counsellor who offers a lot of advice is asking for the client to become dependent. Eventually, of course, some of the advice turns out to be wrong and the spell is broken: the counsellor is seen to be 'only human' and no longer the necessary lifeline perceived by the client in the past. Disenchantment quickly follows and the client/counsellor relationship tends to degenerate rapidly. It is better, then, not to become an advice-giver in the first place.

There are exceptions to this principle where giving advice is appropriate – advice about caring for wounds, taking medication and health education for example. In the sphere of personal problems, however, giving advice is rarely appropriate. Sartre (1973) notes with some irony, that we tend to seek out people who we think will give us a certain sort of advice, the sort that we would tend to give ourselves! A further indication, perhaps, that it is better to enable the client to formulate their own advice rather than our supplying it.

Different personal worlds of client and counsellor

The fact that we have had varied experiences, have different physiologies and differing belief and value systems means that we perceive the world through different frames of reference. We tend to act according to our particular belief about how the world is.

83

What happens next, however, is dependent upon how the world really is. If there is a considerable gap between our personal theory of the world and how the world actually is, we may be disappointed or shocked by the outcome of our actions. We may experience dissonance between what we believe to be the case and what actually is.

It is important that the counsellor realizes that her own belief system may not be shared by the client and the client may not see the world as she does. This is a basic starting point for the development of empathy in the relationship. To try to enter the frame of reference of the client accurately is one of the most important aspects of the relationship. It may also be one of the hardest, for we are always being invaded by our own thoughts, feelings, beliefs and values as we counsel.

A useful starting point is for the counsellor to explore her own belief and value systems before she starts. Simon *et al.* (1978) offer a series of useful exercises in values clarification. It is often surprising how contradictory and inconsistent our belief and value systems are! Once we are able to face some of these contradictions, we may be better able to face the contradictions in the client.

The counsellor's task is to attempt to enter and share the personal world of the client. That view usually changes as counselling progresses (Rogers and Dymond, 1978), after which the client may no longer feel the need for the counsellor. When this happens, the counsellor must develop her own strategies for coping with the separation that usually follows. Counselling is a two-way process. While the client's personal world usually changes, so may the counsellor's. The counselling relationship can, then, be an opportunity for growth and change for the counsellor as well as for the client.

Listening is the basis of the counselling relationship

To really listen to another person is the most caring act of all and takes skill and practice. Often when we claim to be listening, we are busy rehearsing our next verbal response, losing attention and failing to hear the other person. Listening involves giving ourselves up completely to the other person in order to fully understand them.

We cannot listen properly if we are constantly judging or categorizing what we hear. We must learn to set aside our own beliefs and values and to suspend judgement. We must also learn to develop **free-floating attention** – the ability to listen to the changing ebb and flow of the client's verbalizations and not to rush to pull them back to a particular topic. In this sense, what the client is talking about now is what is important. It is a process of offering free attention; of accepting, totally, the other person's story, accepting that their version of how the world is may be different but just as valid as our own.

We need to listen to the metaphors, the descriptions, the value judgements and the words that the client uses: they are all indicators of their personal world. So too, are facial expressions, body movements, eye contact (or lack of it) and other aspects of nonverbal communication.

Counselling techniques should not be overused

If we arm ourselves with a whole battery of counselling techniques, perhaps learned through workshops and courses, we stand to run into problems. The counsellor who uses too many techniques may be perceived by the client as artificial, cold and even uncaring. Perhaps we have all encountered the neophyte counsellor whose determined eye contact and stilted questions make us feel distinctly uncomfortable! It is possible to pay so much attention to techniques that they impede listening and communication.

Some techniques, such as the use of questions, reflections, summary, probing and so forth, are very valuable. They must, however, be used discretely and the human side of the counsellor must show through the techniques at all times. In the end, it is the quality of the relationship that is more important than any techniques that may be used.

Counselling can be learned

Counselling, arguably, is not something that comes naturally to some and not to others. We can all develop listening skills and the ability to communicate clearly with other people, which is the basis of effective counselling. The skills can be learned through personal experience and lots of practice, which may be gained in experiential–learning workshops for the development of counselling skills and through the actual process of doing counselling.

The list of principles offered here is not claimed to be exhaustive. It attempts to identify some of the important principles involved and to explain them. The next task will be to consider the process of the counselling relationship and to identify some of the stages that the relationship passes through as the client explores his world.

BASIC PRINCIPLES AND CONSIDERATIONS IN COUNSELLING IN THE HEALTH PROFESSIONS

The degree to which the issues identified previously will fit with a particular health profession will vary according to the nature of the role of those professionals. For the physiotherapist, for example, the need to give clear and exact information may often be more of a priority than talking through emotional problems. For the nurse working with elderly people, the role of listening and of listening to relatives may play a large part in the overall caring role. Given the different sorts of professional relationships that abound in the professions, it is important to modify the principles discussed in this chapter accordingly. Having said that, the principles apply fairly broadly to almost all relationships in one way or another. They need to be linked, also, to the maps of the counselling relationship discussed in the next chapter and the counselling skills outlined in the following chapters.

5

Maps of the counselling relationship

Two counselling relationships can never be the same. As we have noted, we all come to counselling, whether as counsellor or as client – from different backgrounds and life experiences. Having said that, it may be helpful to sketch out in broad detail the possible nature of a typical counselling relationship. To this end, we need a **map** that can help us to explore the changing course of what happens between counsellor and client. Like any map, it is never the same as the territory itself. If we consider, for instance, the map of the London underground system, it bears no geographical relationship to the actual layout of the rail network. More importantly, though, it gets us around London! So it may be with a map of the counselling process. It may never match exactly what happens in counselling, but it can help us to move through the relationship with greater ease.

Three different sorts of maps are offered here. The first is an eight-stage model that considers the changing and developing nature of the relationship. The second offers a very practical method of structuring the counselling process. The third considers three dimensions of counselling as a means of evaluating the relationship as it develops. The three can be used in various ways. First, one can be chosen as a way of working in counselling – the map is chosen by the counsellor as the preferred one to be used in everyday practice, rather in the way that a person may use an AA map in preference to an Ordnance Survey map. Alternatively, any combination of the three may be used to highlight different aspects of counselling. The first, for example, may give a general overview of the whole relationship. The second may offer a practical set of steps that can be worked through. The third may highlight various aspects of counselling work that must be considered at various points throughout the relationship. The maps are not mutually exclusive: they all relate to the same thing and can be used together.

AN EIGHT-STAGE MAP OF THE COUNSELLING RELATIONSHIP

The stages in the model are enumerated below. It is suggested that this model offers a broad overview of how the relationship, typically, will unfold. Now not all relationships will necessarily pass through each of the stages: some will reach certain stages and not others. Other relationships will by-pass certain of the stages. The aim of the map is to offer a broad overview of the sorts of potential stages that many relationships will move through.

Stage one: meeting the client
Stage two: discussion of surface issues
Stage three: revelation of deeper issues
Stage four: ownership of feelings and possibly, emotional release
Stage five: generation of insight: the client's life is viewed by them in a different light
Stage six: problem-solving future planning
Stage seven: action by the client
Stage eight: disengagement from the counselling relationship by the client

Stage one: meeting the client

In this first stage, the client meets the counsellor for the first time. Each is sounding out the other and setting tacit ground rules for the relationship. In a sense, both client and counsellor are 'on their best behaviour'. This is an important part of the larger counselling relationship in that it sets the tone for the whole dialogue. The skilled counsellor will set the client at ease in this stage and encourage him to gently spell out his reasons for talking to the counsellor. It is likely that both parties will experience some anxiety in this phase of the relationship: the client will want to be seen in a good light by the counsellor and the counsellor will be keen to ensure that the client feels comfortable in her company.

88

Stage two: discussion of surface issues

As the relationship slowly unfolds, the client will begin to tell his story or identify his problems in living. These will usually start with 'safe' disclosures: the deeper issues will reveal themselves later. Murray Cox (1978) offers a useful device for identifying the level of disclosure in the counselling relationship. He distinguishes between three levels of self-disclosure by the client: first, second and third levels. First-level disclosures are safe and relatively unimportant disclosures. Examples of first-level disclosures will vary according to the context but examples may be:

It took me a long time to get here today.
It took me a long time to find your office.
I haven't been to this part of the town before.

These are usually fairly polite statements that act as 'feelers' in relationship. They serve to test out the relationship in terms of trust and confidence. As the relationship deepens, so the level of self-disclosure increases. Levels two and three of Cox's model are in the following stage.

Stage three: revelation of deeper issues

Level two of Cox's (1978) model refers to the disclosure of feelings. Again, such disclosures will depend on the individual and the context but examples of such second-level disclosures may be:

I feel really angry about that.
I find it very difficult to feel positive about anything.
I'm not happy when I'm at home.

Second-level disclosures will not occur until the relationship between counsellor and client is sufficiently developed to the point where the client feels confident and trusting with the counsellor. It is a significant indicator that the relationship has deepened when the client begins to offer disclosure of how he is feeling.

Third-level disclosures are those that indicate the really deep, existential concerns of the client – the sorts of things that they may not have disclosed to any other person or have disclosed to very few people. If you stop reading for a moment and think of two things that very few people know about you, those would be third-level disclosures if you revealed them to another person. A clear principle emerges here: the client's potential third-level issues are not necessarily the same as the counsellor's third-level issues and vice versa. There is considerable danger in being misunderstood and in misunderstanding if we forget this. There is a temptation to believe that what troubles us is what troubles most people.

On the other hand, there is a certain paradox arising at this point, for as Rogers (1967) notes: 'What is most personal is most general'. Some of the most difficult things to talk about turn out to be difficult for all of us. There is a certain commonality of human experience that makes it the case that we all share certain fundamental difficulties. However, we would be wrong to assume that it is necessarily true that what I as a counsellor worry about, my clients worry about. Identification with the client is perhaps the most difficult issue here. We must be careful to draw the boundaries between ourselves and the client himself if we are to allow the latter to express his own third-level issues in his own time. It is arguable, too, that we will not allow the client to make third-level disclosures until we are accepting enough and comfortable with ourselves. We can easily and unconsciously put the client in the position of not being able to make these profound disclosures by our being defensive. To really listen to another person talking of their deeper human concerns is often a difficult business. This is yet another reason why we should as counsellors, develop self-awareness, it may be only when we have faced some of our own third-level problems that we will allow the client to discuss his.

Third-level disclosures are often heralded by certain changes in the client. He may become more quiet, his facial expression may change and eye contact may be less sustained. If the person is disclosing something that has taken him considerable courage to disclose, that disclosure is bound to be accompanied by considerable anxiety. Often, if the counsellor sits quietly and attentively, the client will make the disclosure. If the counsellor is too talkative or questioning, the disclosure may be avoided all together. The timing of third-level disclosures, by the client, is fairly critical and if the circumstances of the relationship are not optimal, the disclosure may be postponed or never made at all. Once a third-level disclosure *has* been made, all that is often necessary is for the counsellor to sit and listen to the client as he struggles to make sense of what has happened. Little intervention is needed at this point and the counsellor should avoid the temptation to 'overtalk' the client because of her own anxiety at

Figure 5.1 The rhythm of counselling (based on M. Cox, 1978).

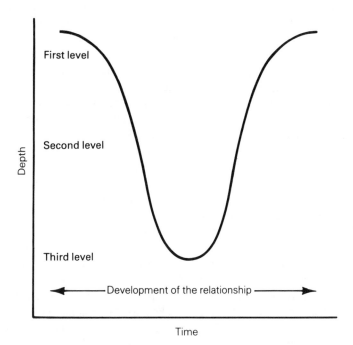

being offered the disclosure (Heron, 1986).

Examples of typical third-level disclosures are difficult to describe. More than any other sort, they tend to be idiosyncratic and defined by the context of the relationship. Many are metaphorical in nature. For example, the client may say: 'I never really had a childhood' or 'I realize that I have never felt anything really'. Others are more direct:

I've never loved my wife.
I hated my parents more than anything else.
I'm homosexual.

Third-level disclosures do not occur all together: they tend to be made at various points throughout the counselling relationship. Figure 5.1 demonstrates what may be termed the **rhythm of counselling** – the cycle of disclosures that starts with level one, deepens to level two and deepens, still further to level three. It then, typically, lightens again and the client gradually returns to less difficult topics. Then the cycle starts again and the relationship deepens again. It may be important that this changing of level from deeper to lighter occurs. Too much disclosure, too quickly, can lead to the client feeling embarrassed and very deep disclosure made much too quickly can lead to the client returning only to first-level disclosures, never to return to the more profound issues. Indeed, such sudden deep disclosure may lead to the client's subsequent withdrawal from the relationship altogether. Having made this very sudden disclosure, the client leaves feeling embarrassed and finds it difficult to return to face the counsellor again.

If such sudden, deep disclosure seems imminent at the beginning of a counselling relationship, it is sometimes sensible to lighten the conversation and allow the disclosure rate to slow down. In this way, the client discloses more gently and stands to feel more comfortable in the following sessions.

Third-level disclosures would seem to be an important part of the counselling process. The very fact that a client can articulate some of his deeper fears, anxieties and problems means that the possibility of resolving them is more likely. Also, the process of self-disclosure can often serve to change the client's perceptions of his problems. A considerable amount of energy is taken up with holding onto these more profound problems. The disclosure of them is often accompanied by a great sense of relief.

Clearly, third-level disclosures need to be received and heard by the counsellor with great tact. It is important that the client does not feel patronized or judged after such a disclosure. The very process of disclosure, itself, has been difficult enough, without the counsellor making the person feel more uncomfortable. As we have seen, the counsellor is often required to do nothing but listen. Also, too, the disclosure may be followed by a period of silence on the part of the client as he pieces together his thoughts on what he has said.

Stage four: ownership of feelings and possible emotional release

When the client has begun to talk about the very profound problems of his life, the tone of the dialogue will often change in a very significant way. The client stops talking about feelings that he has in a general, or detached sort of way and begins to experience the feelings themselves. In other words, the feelings begin to accompany the conversation. This can be described as **ownership** of those feelings. An example of the change in emotional state is illustrated in the following passage: 'Sometimes... sometimes when I'm at home, I get quite angry with various members of the family...' and 'Something odd is happening... I'm feeling angry now... I'm really furious! I won't be treated like that! It's my son, David... I'm really mad with him...'. The change can be quite dramatic as the client begins to thaw out and experience the feelings that he may have been bottling up for a considerable period. Sometimes the switch to experiencing the feelings as they are talked about is only transitory and the client quickly switches back to the safety of talking in the abstract. Sometimes, however, the sense of experiencing the feeling leads to more profound release of emotion. Thus, as the feelings are experienced, the person expresses those emotions through tears, anger, or fear – cathartic release. Sometimes, too, the embarrassment of the sudden realization of feeling leads to expression of that feeling in the form of laughter (Heron, 1977a). This embarrassed laughter may quickly tip over into tears, anger or fear. Again, the counsellor's role, here, is to allow the expression of feelings, the cathartic release. The tears, anger or fear may last for a few moments or may be sustained. The longer the counsellor can refrain from jumping to rescue the client from their feelings, the more likely it is that the client will benefit from the release.

Stage five: generation of insight: the client's life is viewed by them in a different light

It would seem that cathartic release generates insight (Heron, 1977b). If we can allow the expression of pent-up feeling and not interrupt that expression or attempt to interpret it, the client will come to view their life situation differently. It is as though the expression of pent-up feeling releases in the client a natural ability to think more rationally and see things more clearly. Often all that is required in this stage is to sit quietly as the client experiences that insight and verbalizes it. There is, of course, no reason to suppose that the client will necessarily verbalize the insights gained through cathartic release but their nonverbal behaviour will usually indicate that the client is piecing the insights together. Often they will sit looking away from the counsellor, clearly thinking deeply. The temptation is often to interrupt that process with a series of questions but as a general rule, the process is best left undisturbed. The gain in insight is usually greater if the client can be allowed the time and space to appreciate it.

Figure 5.2 A problem-solving cycle.

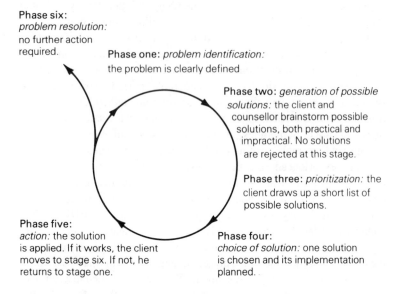

Phase six:
problem resolution:
no further action
required.

Phase one: *problem identification:*
the problem is clearly defined

Phase two: *generation of possible
solutions:* the client and
counsellor brainstorm possible
solutions, both practical and
impractical. No solutions
are rejected at this stage.

Phase three: *prioritization:* the
client draws up a short list of
possible solutions.

Phase five:
action: the solution
is applied. If it works, the client
moves to stage six. If not, he
returns to stage one.

Phase four:
choice of solution: one solution
is chosen and its implementation
planned.

Stage six: problem-solving/future planning

The expression of pent-up emotion and the insight gained through its
release are not enough in themselves. The client still has to consider
ways in which he is going to use that insight to change certain
aspects of his life. Thus, once the tears have been shed and the
perceptual shift has occurred, the client is often helped by the use
of a practical problem-solving cycle (Burnard, 1985). Figure 5.2
offers one such cycle. In phase one, the problem is clearly defined.
This comes about through talking through the client's situation
carefully and helping them to express what they see as the problem
as concisely as they can. In the second phase, the client and the
counsellor generate as many possible solutions to that problem as
they can. This process is sometimes known as **brainstorming** and
involves considering every possibility, both rational and sensible and
the more bizarre! Such a process can open up a fruitful and creative
series of possible solutions that a plainly logical approach may not.

In phase three, a short list of possible solutions is drawn up and
in stage four, the client makes a decision about which solution he
will choose. Next, that solution is put into operation in the client's
life and, if it works, the problem is resolved. If it does not, the

problem-solving cycle can be worked through again, perhaps with a clearer definition of the problem.

Stage seven: action

As we noted at the outset, counselling must have a practical end. In this case, as the client comes to identify his problems of living, talk them through with the counsellor, express pent-up emotion and identify solutions, it is important that he introduces changes in his life. Indeed, if no such changes take place, the counselling is of very little use. This **action** stage of the relationship takes place away from the counsellor/client meetings and consists of the client trying new ways of living. During this stage, the client will obviously need a considerable amount of support from the counsellor but essentially, this will be the client's independent aspect of the relationship. It will also involve a growing independence on the part of the client who comes to realize that they can live without the counsellor and can make life choices without the counsellor's help. This stage shades into the next.

Stage eight: disengagement from the counselling process

This is what it says. Gradually, or sometimes abruptly, the client feels more and more able to cope on his own. Thus, the counselling relationship comes to an end. This may create considerable anxieties in both counsellor and client. The relationship has developed into a close one and to some degree, both people have become dependent on each other. The skilled counsellor is one who can effectively help in the disengagement process and not require the client to remain attached to her. This is the ultimate act of altruism, perhaps. It is the process of saying goodbye, with no strings attached. The goodbye must be unequivocal and without regret or remorse. The counsellor has completed her task and the client has learned to live for himself and with himself. Often, old issues of separation come to the fore, here. Bowlby (1975) wrote of 'separation anxiety' – the anxiety some people feel when they find a relationship coming to an end. Bowlby hypothesized that such people had experienced difficulties in early separations – in childhood or even in early infancy. Here, again, we find the need for the counsellor's developing self-awareness and the need for her to explore any identified difficulties with separations and with the ends of counselling relationships. It is important that such partings are smooth and that both parties are comfortable with the ending.

A THREE-STAGE MODEL OF THE COUNSELLING RELATIONSHIP

The second map for guidance in the process of counselling is Egan's (1986b) three-stage model of the helping relationship. His three stages are:

1. identifying and clarifying problem situations
2. goal-setting: developing and choosing preferred scenarios
3. action: moving towards the preferred scenario

In stage one, the counsellor helps the client to tell his story – to explore his present life situation as he sees it now. Out of that story emerges the specific problems of living that could not have been identified prior to this exploratory process. It is as if the very telling of the story brings out the problems and puts a name to them. Egan notes also, that this stage is useful for exploring 'blind spots' – aspects of the client's life that he had not considered.

In stage two, the client is helped to imagine a possible future situation that would be preferable to the present one. Initially, this often means imagining a variety of possible future scenarios, out of which the client slowly homes in on one. Once this realistic scenario has been discussed, the client and counsellor can identify goals that can help in the achievement of the proposed future state.

In stage three, the client and counsellor devise ways in which the proposed future scenario is achieved. In the first instance, this can be aided by the process of brainstorming, as described above. All possible methods of achieving the desired outcome are identified and then, gradually, a particular approach is chosen out of all the possibilities. Then, an action plan is drawn up in order to aid the achievement of the desired scenario further. The final substage of stage three is action on the part of the client – the time when the client makes the discussion concrete and puts the plan into action, supported by the counsellor.

Egan's (1986b) three-stage model can serve as a useful and practical map in counselling and a means of bringing structure to the process of counselling. The three stages, although interrelated, can be dealt with as separate aspects of counselling and thus the relationship takes shape and has specific goals. Keeping the three stages in mind can help the counsellor to assess where the relationship is going and how it is developing. Obviously, no time limit can be put on how long each of the stages may take to work through with any given person but using them can ensure that the relationship remains dynamic and forward-moving.

Egan's model in practice

June is an occupational therapist working with a group of young patients in a small psychiatric day hospital. She is approached by one patient, Alice, a girl recently discharged from hospital where she was treated for anorexia nervosa. Alice says that she wants to talk but is unclear about what her problems are.

June uses Egan's three-stage model and allows Alice to describe everything that is happening to her at the present time. Thus, a picture of Alice's life emerges. Out of this picture, Alice identifies two problem areas: her overdependent relationship with her mother and her lack of self-confidence. June asks her to clarify how she would like the future to be. Alice talks of greater independence from her mother and an enhanced ability to socialize and mix more easily.

Out of their discussion, June and Alice draw up a list of practical, manageable tasks for the immediate future, including:

1. Alice to set aside time to talk to her mother
2. Alice to consider the practicality of finding a flat or bedsitter near her parents' home
3. Alice and June to work out a social-skills training programme for Alice to follow with a group of other day-hospital clients
4. Alice to attend a weekend workshop on assertiveness-training at a local college

THREE DIMENSIONS OF THE COUNSELLING RELATIONSHIP

Yet another way of mapping the relationship is in terms of three dimensions: time, depth and mutuality (Cox, 1978). Again, although each dimension overlaps with the other and is dependent on the other, each may be considered separately.

Time

The concept of time in the counselling relationship can be understood in at least two ways. First, there is the logical structuring of the counselling relationship itself. It makes sense for the counsellor to suggest a well-defined period of time for the counsellor/client meeting. Setting a boundary in this way has many advantages: once set, it can be forgotten about by both counsellor and client. Both know how long they will be together and when the session will finish. In an open-ended session, both may be confused about how long the session will last. A stated contract of, say, an hour overcomes this problem. The contract also means that the client will tend to use the time available constructively. As we have already noted, the client will often disclose important information towards the end of the meeting. If he does not know when that end will come, he may never make the disclosure. Also, an unstructured session may be fine when the counsellor is not busy but when constraints of work mean that the counselling session has to be truncated, the client may feel rejected. On balance, then, it seems better to structure the time more formally at the outset.

A second, more subtle aspect of time-structuring relates to the focus of the counselling in terms of past, present and future. These three aspects may be considered as follows:

1. Past – the client's past, personal history
2. Present – the client's present situation and the present situation for the client and counsellor together
3. Future – the client's aspirations, plans and hopes for what is to come

In counselling those with emotional or psychological problems, it may be useful to consider spending roughly equal time in discussing all three time zones.

Our past experience has much to do with how we view the present. Indeed, what we are in the present may be seen as having grown out of past experience. Both past and present experience will determine, to a greater or lesser extent, how we make use of the future. Some people seem to want to live in the past; perhaps it was more comfortable or acceptable. Others look forward to what may happen in the future and dismiss the past as irrelevant – so much 'water under the bridge'. Tomorrow will always be better than today. Both living in the past and living for the future are, perhaps, unrealistic. To live in the present, with a strong sense of both past and future may be more useful and constructive.

A balanced counselling relationship may take into account all three of these aspects of time. The counsellor may want to ask how the present situation is affected by past events and how the client views the future, given the present climate. If past, present and future are addressed in roughly equal amounts, then the momentum of the relationship remains continuous. There is a sense of continuity running through the relationship.

Depth

The second dimension in this map is depth. This refers to the aspects of intimacy and personal disclosure in the relationship and it depends on the amount of time invested in it. Depth cannot be hurried. It evolves out of the feeling of trust engendered by the client–counsellor process, but it does seem to develop in a cyclical manner. At the beginning of the relationship (and at the beginning of each counselling hour), there is usually a discussion of superficial things (first-level disclosures). As the relationship and the hour develop, so the depth of the relationship increases (through second- and third-level disclosures). The client slowly reveals himself to the counsellor and discloses more and more. Towards the end of the relationship (and the hour), the atmosphere lightens and the counselling relationship moves once again to a more superficial note. Thus, the use of Cox's (1978) three levels of disclosure may be used to assess the depth of the relationship, both on a session-to-session basis and from the point of a longer term relationship.

Many factors determine the depth of the relationship. A short list would include the counsellor's ability to empathize with the client, the counsellor's range of skills, the personalities and temperaments of counsellor and client, the degree of 'match' between the two people and the prevailing moods of both people.

Mutuality

The third dimension of structure is mutuality. This refers to the client's and counsellor's shared relationship with each other. As we noted earlier (p. 72), Martin Buber referred to the 'I–thou' relationship – the natural unfolding of relationship between two people who know each other on a reasonably equal and intimate level. Carl Rogers (1967) described the process of emerging from what resembled a hypnotic trance at the end of the counselling session. This trancelike state reflects the close nature of the truly mutual client–counsellor relationship. Everything outside the relationship is forgotten while the client and counsellor are together – a close bonding occurs.

How does such mutuality develop? Arguably, it arises out of shared experiences and self-disclosure (although limits to this are discussed above). The counselling relationship, far from being a one-way traffic of disclosure from the client to the counsellor, becomes a time when human experiences are pooled. This is not to say that the counsellor should burden the client with her own problems, but to acknowledge that 'disclosure begets disclosure' (Jourard, 1964). I feel more understood when the person to whom I am talking shares something of their own experience with me.

To develop mutuality, the counsellor has to develop an open, nondefensive and transparent presentation of self. Rather than hiding behind a professional mask, they allow themselves to be seen as they are – warts and all! It is worth noting that professionals who allow themselves to make mistakes occasionally are generally sensed as far more approachable and human than are their highly skilled perfect counterparts. It would seem that fallability is a necessary prerequisite of good counselling.

If this mutuality is missing, then the counselling process will remain superficial. If the counsellor always presents a professional facade and never allows the client to know her, then mutuality cannot develop. Mutuality is a measure both of the depth of the relationship and of the counsellor's commitment to the relationship. It develops out of the counsellor's life experience, ability to empathize, skill and genuine commitment to the task.

These, then, are three ways of mapping out the counselling relationship. They differ in approach and degree of detail and perhaps they will appeal to different sorts of counsellors. Whilst no map is essential to counselling, some structure can help the unfamiliar to look a little less frightening. It can also suggest the direction forward and, at best, counselling should always be a dynamic and evolving process, though, at times – like life itself – it will become stuck! Often, it is these periods of being stuck that are some of the most important. If we can stand to stay with the stuckness and even to abandon the map, the result for the client in the long term can be much more rewarding.

MAPS OF THE COUNSELLING RELATIONSHIP AND THE HEALTH PROFESSIONAL

What map a particular health professional chooses in order to bring structure to their counselling will depend to a degree on the time available and the nature of the relationship. Where time is limited and a reasonable amount of resolution of a problem must be achieved, Egan's (1986b) three-stage model is excellent. It is practical, structured and allows both health professional and client to see where the relationship is going and how it is progressing. Those professionals concerned with longer term relationships may choose the first and third models described in this chapter, for they emphasize, more, the processes that occur in the development of the counselling relationship. None of the maps, however, is mutually exclusive. Any of the maps may be used in conjunction with any of the others and combined with the use of effective counselling skills described in the following chapters.

101

6

Counselling skills I: listening and attending

Listening and attending are by far the most important aspects of the counselling process. Often the best counselling is that which involves the counsellor only listening to the other person. Unfortunately, most of us feel that we are obliged of talk! Unfortunately, too, it is over-talking by the counsellor that is least productive. If we can train ourselves to give our full attention to the other person and really listen, we can do much to help them. First, we need to discriminate between the two processes – attending and listening.

ATTENDING

Attending is the act of truly focusing on the other person. It involves consciously making ourselves aware of what the other person is saying and of what they are trying to communicate to us. Figure 6.1 demonstrates three hypothetical zones of attention. The zones may help to further clarify this concept of attending and have implications for improving the quality of attention offered to the client.

Zone 1, in Figure 6.1, represents the zone of having our attention fully focused outside of ourselves and on the environment around us or, in the context of counselling, on the client. When we have our attention fully focused 'out' in this way, we are fully aware of the other person and not distracted by our own thoughts and feelings.

There are some simple activities, borrowed from the practice of meditation, that can help and enhance our ability to offer this sort of attention. Here is a particularly straightforward one. Stop reading this book for a moment and allow your attention to focus on an object in the room that you are in – it may be a clock, or a picture or a piece of furniture – anything. Focus your attention on the object

Figure 6.1 Three possible zones of attention.

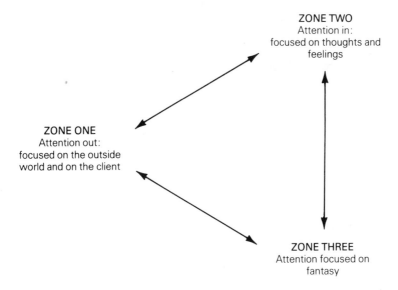

and notice every aspect of it – its shape, its colour, its size and so forth. Continue to do this for at least one minute. Notice as you do this, how your attention becomes fully absorbed by the object. You have focused your attention out. Then discontinue your close observation. Notice what is going on in your mind. What are your thoughts and feelings at the moment? When you do this, you shift your attention to zone two, the internal domain of thoughts and feelings. Now shift the focus of your attention out again and onto another object. Study every aspect of it for about a minute. Notice, as you do this, how it is possible to consciously and awarely shift the focus of your attention in this way. You can will yourself to focus your attention outside of yourself. Practice at this conscious process will improve your ability to fully focus attention outside of yourself and onto the client.

Clearly, if we are to pay close attention to every aspect of the client, it is important to be able to move freely between zones one and two. In practice, what probably happens in a counselling session is that we spend some time in zone one paying full attention to the client and then we shuttle back into zone two and notice our reactions, feelings and beliefs about what they are saying before we shift our attention back out. The important thing is that we learn to gain

103

control over this process. It is no longer a haphazard, hit-and-miss affair, but we can learn to focus attention with some precision. It is not until we train ourselves to consciously focus attention 'out' in this way that we can really notice what the other person is saying and doing.

Zone three in Figure 6.1 involves fantasy – ideas and beliefs that we have that bear no direct relation to what is going on at the moment but concerns what we think or believe is going on. When we listen to another person, it is quite possible to think and believe all sorts of things about them. We may, for example, think 'I know what he's really trying to tell me. He's trying to say that he doesn't want to go back to work, only he won't admit it – even to himself!' When we engage in this sort of internal dialogue, we are working within the domain of fantasy. We cannot know other things about people, unless we ask them, or as Epting puts it: 'If you want to know what another person is about, ask them, they might just tell you!' (Epting, 1984). We often think that we do know what other people think or feel, without checking with that person first. If we do this, it is because we are focusing on the zone of fantasy: we are engaged in the processes of attribution or interpretation. The problem with these sorts of processes is that, if they are wrong, we stand to develop a very distorted picture of the other person! Our assumptions naturally lead us to other assumptions and if we begin to ask questions directly generated by those assumptions, our counselling will lack clarity and our client will end up being very confused!

A useful rule, then, is that if we find ourselves within the domain of fantasy and we are inventing things about the person in front of us, we stop and if necessary, check those inventions with the client to test the validity of them. If the client confirms them, all well and good: we have intuitively picked up something about the client that he was, perhaps, not consciously or overtly telling us. If, on the other hand, we are wrong, it is probably best to abandon the fantasy all together. The fantasy, invention or assumption probably tells us more about our own mental make-up than it does about that of our client! In fact, these wrong assumptions can serve to help us gain more self-awareness. In noticing the wrong assumptions we make about others, we can reflect on what those assumptions tell us about ourselves.

Awareness of the focus of attention and its shift between the three zones has implications for all aspects of counselling. The counsellor who is able to keep attention directed out for long periods is likely to be more observant and more accurate than the counsellor who is not. The counsellor who can discriminate between the zone of thinking and the zone of fantasy is less likely to jump to conclusions about their observations or to make value judgements based on interpretation rather than on fact.

What is being suggested here is that we learn to focus directly on the other person (zone one) with occasional moves to the domain of our own thoughts and feelings (zone two) but that we learn, also, to attempt to avoid the domain of fantasy (zone three). It is almost as though we learn to meet the client as a 'blank slate': we know little about them until they tell us who they are. To work in this way in counselling is, almost paradoxically, a much more empathic way of working. We learn rapidly not to assume things about the other person but to listen to them and to check out any hunches or intuitions we may have about them.

Being able to focus on zone one and have our attention focused out has other advantages. First, by focusing in this way, we can learn to maintain the therapeutic distance referred to in Chapter 4 (p. 79). We can learn to distinguish clearly between what are the client's problems and what are our own. It is only when we become mixed up by having our attention partly focused on the client, partly on our own thoughts and feelings and partly on our fantasies and interpretations that we begin to get confused about what the client is telling us and what we are saying to ourselves. We easily confuse our own problems with those of the client.

Second, we can use the concept of the three domains of attention to develop self-awareness. By noticing the times when we have great difficulty in focusing attention out, we can learn to notice points of stress and difficulty in our own lives. Typically, we will find it difficult to focus attention out when we are tired, under pressure or emotionally distressed. The lack of attention that we experience can come to serve as a signal that we need to stop and take stock of our own life situation. Further, by allowing ourselves consciously to focus in on zones two and three – the process of introspection – we can examine our thoughts and feelings in order to further understand our own make-up. Indeed, this process of self-exploration seems to be essential if we are to be able to offer another person sustained attention. If we constantly bottle up problems, we will find ourselves distracted by what the client has to say. Typically, when they begin to talk of a problem of theirs that is also a problem for us, we will suddenly find our attention distracted to zone two: suddenly we will find ourselves pondering on our own problems and not those of the client! Regular self-examination can help to clear away, at least temporarily, some of the more pressing personal problems that we experience. A case, perhaps of 'counsellor, counsel thyself!'

Such exploration can be carried out either in isolation, in pairs or in groups. The skills exercises in Chapter 11 offer practical suggestions as to how such exploration can be developed. If done in isolation, meditative techniques can be of value. Often, however, the preference will be to conduct such exploration in pairs or groups. In this way, we gain further insight through hearing other people's thoughts, feelings and observations and we can make useful comparisons between other people's experience and our own. There are a variety of formats for running self-awareness groups, including sensitivity groups, encounter groups, group therapy and training groups. Such groups are often organized by colleges and extra-mural departments of universities but they can also be set up on a 'do-it-yourself' basis. Ernst and Goodison (1981) offer some particularly useful guidelines for setting up, running and maintaining a self-help group for self-help exploration. Such a group is useful as a means of developing self-awareness, as a peer-support group for talking through counselling problems and also as a means for developing further counselling skills. Trying out new skills in a safe and trusting environment is often a better proposition than trying them out with real clients!

Attending in practice

Elizabeth, a health visitor, finds that during a busy day it is difficult to cut off from one of her clients before visiting another. She finds herself preoccupied with the problems of a previous visit during a visit to another person. Through practising the process of focusing attention out between visits and by taking a few minutes in her car to disassociate from the client she has just visited, she develops the skill of giving full attention to the next person she sees.

LISTENING

Listening is the process of hearing the other person. This involves not only noting the things that they say but also a whole range of other aspects of communication. Figure 6.2 outlines some of the things that can be noted during listening. Given the wide range of ways in which one person tries to communicate with another, this is

Figure 6.2 Three aspects of listening.

Linguistic aspects
– words
– phrases
– metaphors
etc.

Paralinguistic aspects
– timing
– volume
– pitch
– accent
– 'ums and errs'
– fluency
etc.

Nonverbal aspects of communication
– facial expression
– use of gesture
– touch
– body position
– proximity to the counsellor
– body movement
– eye contact
etc.

---

further evidence of the need to develop the ability to offer close and sustained attention, as outlined previously. Three aspects of listening are noted in the diagram. **Linguistic** aspects of speech refer to the actual words that the client uses, to the phrases they choose and to the metaphors they use to convey how they are feeling. Attention to such metaphors is often useful as metaphorical language can often convey more than can conventional use of language (Cox, 1978). **Paralinguistics** refers to all those aspects of speech that are not words themselves. Thus, timing, volume, pitch, accent are all para-linguistic aspects of communication. Again, they can offer us indicators of how the other person is feeling beyond the words that they use. Again, however, we must be careful of making assumptions and slipping into zone three, the zone of fantasy (see p. 104). Paralinguistics can only offer us a possible clue to how the other person is feeling. It is important that we check with the client the degree to which that clue matches with the client's own perception of the way he feels.

Nonverbal aspects of communication refer to body language: the way that the client expresses himself through the use of his body. Thus facial expression, use of gestures, body position and movement, proximity to the counsellor, touch in relation to the counsellor, all offer further clues about the client's internal status beyond the words he uses and can be listened to by the attentive counsellor. Again, any assumptions that we make about what such body language means need to be clarified with the client. There is a temptation to believe that body language can be read, as if we all used it in the same sort of way. This is, perhaps, encouraged by such works as Desmond Morris's (1978) *Manwatching*. Reflection on the subject, however, will reveal that body language is dependent to a large degree on a wide number of variables – the context in which it occurs, the nature of the relationship, the individual's personal style and preference, the personality of the person using the body language, and so on. It is safer, therefore, not to assume that we know what another person is saying with their body language but again, to treat it as a clue and to clarify with the client what he means by his use of it. Thus it is preferable, in counselling, to merely bring to the client's attention the way he is sitting, or his facial expression, rather than to offer an interpretation of it. Two examples may help here. In the first, the counsellor is offering an interpretation and an assumption: 'I notice from the way that you have your arms folded and from your frown that you are uncomfortable with discussing things at home.' In the second example, the counsellor merely feeds back to the client what she observes and allows the client to clarify his situation: 'I notice that you have your arms folded and that you're frowning. What are you feeling at the moment?'

Levels of listening

The skilled counsellor learns to listen to all three aspects of communication and tries to resist the temptation to interpret what she hears. Three levels of listening may be identified (Figure 6.3).

The first level of listening refers to the idea of the counsellor merely noting what is being said. In this mode, neither client nor counsellor are psychologically very close and arguably the relationship will not develop very much. In the second level of listening, the

Figure 6.3 Three levels of listening.

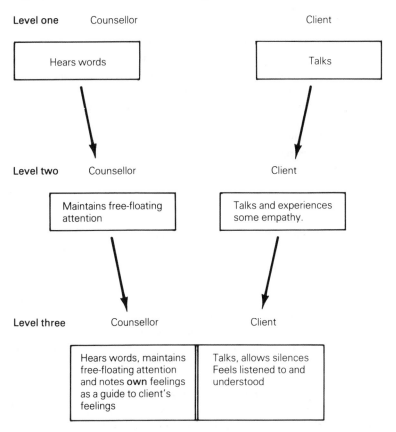

counsellor learns to develop free-floating attention. That is to say that she listens overall to what is being said, as opposed to trying to catch every word. Free-floating attention also refers to going with the client, of not trying to keep the client to a particular theme but of following the client's conversation wherever it goes. She also 'listens' to the client's nonverbal and paralinguistic behaviour as indicators of what the client is thinking and feeling. Faced with this deeper level of listening, the client feels a greater amount of empathy being offered by the counsellor. The counsellor begins to enter the frame of reference of the client and to explore his perceptual world. She begins to see the world as the client experiences it.

In the third level of listening, the counsellor maintains free-floating attention, notices nonverbal and paralinguistic aspects of communication but also notices her own internal thoughts, feelings and body sensations. As Rollo May (1983b) notes, it is frequently the case that what the counsellor is feeling, once the counselling relationship has deepened, is a direct mirror image of what the client is feeling. Thus, the counsellor sensitively notices changes in herself and gently checks these with the client. It is as though the counsellor is listening both to the client and to herself and carefully using herself as a sounding board for how the relationship is developing. Watkins (1978), referring to Carl Rogers, has described this process as **resonance** and points out that this process is different to that of empathizing:

> Rogers says that empathy means *understanding* of the feelings of another. He holds that the therapist does not necessarily himself experience the feelings. If he did, according to Rogers, that would be identification, and this is not the same as empathy. Resonance *is* a type of identification which is temporary.
>
> (Watkins, 1978)

The use of the process of resonance needs to be judged carefully. Whilst it does not involve interpreting or offering a theory about what the client is feeling, it does offer a particularly close form of listening that can make the client feel listened to and fully understood. It is notable, too, that in these circumstances, the client will often feel more comfortable with periods of silence as he struggles to verbalize his thoughts and feelings. Arguably, he allows these silences because he senses that the counsellor is 'with him' more completely than at other levels of listening. The net result of this deeper level of listening is that a truly empathic relationship develops. The client feels listened to, the counsellor feels she is understanding the client and a level of mutuality is achieved in which both people are communicating, both rationally and intuitively.

Use of minimal prompts

Whilst the counsellor is listening to the client, it is important that she shows that she is listening. An obvious aid to this is the use of what may be described as **minimal prompts** – the use of head nods, yes's, mm's and so on. All of these indicate that 'I am with you'. On the other hand, overuse of them can be irritating to the client, particularly, perhaps, the thoughtless and repetitive nodding of the head – the 'dog in the back of the car' phenomenon! It is important that the counsellor, at least initially, is consciously aware of her use of minimal prompts and tries to vary her repertoire. It is important to note also, that very often such prompts are not necessary at all. Often, all the client needs is to be listened to and appreciates that the counsellor is listening without the need for further reinforcement of the fact.

Behavioural aspects of listening

One other consideration needs be made regarding the process of listening and that is the behaviours the counsellor adopts when listening to the client. Egan (1986b) offers the acronym SOLER as a means of identifying and remembering the sorts of counsellor behaviour that encourage effective listening. The acronym is used as follows:

1. Sit Squarely in relation to the client
2. maintain an Open position
3. Lean slightly towards the client
4. maintain reasonable Eye contact with the client
5. Relax

First, the counsellor is encouraged to sit squarely in relation to the client. This can be understood both literally and metaphorically. In North America and the UK, it is generally acknowledged that one person listens to another more effectively if she sits opposite or nearly opposite the other person, rather than next to him. Sitting opposite allows the counsellor to see all aspects of communication, both paralinguistic and nonverbal, that might be missed if she sat next to the client.

Second, the counsellor should consider adopting an open position in relation to the client. Again, this can be understood both literally and metaphorically. A closed attitude is as much a block to effective counselling as is a closed body position. Crossed arms and legs, however, can convey a defensive feeling to the client and counselling is often more effective if the counsellor sits without crossing either. Having said that, many people feel more comfortable sitting with their legs crossed, so perhaps some licence should be used here! What should be avoided is the position where the counsellor sits in

111

a 'knotted' position with both arms and legs crossed.

It is helpful if the counsellor appreciates that they can lean towards the client. This can encourage the client and make them feel more understood. If this does not seem immediately clear, next time you talk to someone, try leaning away from the other person and note the result!

Eye contact with the client should be reasonably sustained and a good rule of thumb is that the amount of eye contact that the counsellor uses should roughly match the amount the client uses. It is important, however, that the counsellor's eyes should be 'available' for the client and the counsellor always prepared to maintain eye contact. On the other hand, it is important that the client does not feel stared at nor intimidated by the counsellor's glare. Conscious use of eye contact can ensure that the client feels listened to and understood but not uncomfortable.

The amount of eye contact the counsellor can make will depend on a number of factors, including the topic under discussion, the degree of comfortableness the counsellor feels with the client, the degree to which the counsellor feels attracted to the client, the amount of eye contact the client makes, the nature and quality of the client's eye contact and so forth. If the counsellor continually finds the maintainance of eye contact difficult, it is, perhaps, useful to consider talking the issue over with a trusted colleague or with a peer-support group, for eye contact is a vital channel of communication in most interpersonal encounters (Heron, 1970).

Finally, it is important that the counsellor feels relaxed while listening. This usually means that she should refrain from rehearsing responses in her head. It means that she should give herself up completely to the task of listening and trust herself to make an appropriate response when she has to. This underlines the need to consider listening as the most important aspect of counselling. Everything else is secondary to it. Many people feel that they have to have a ready response when engaged in a conversation with another person. In counselling, however, the main focus of the conversation is the client. The counsellor's verbal responses, although important, must be secondary to what the client has to say. Thus, all the counsellor has to do is to sit back and listen intently. Easily said but not so easily done! The temptation to overtalk is often great but can lessen with more experience and with the making of a conscious decision not to make too many verbal interventions.

All of these behavioural considerations can help the listening process. In order to be effective, however, they need to be used consciously. The counsellor needs to pay attention to using them and choose to use them. As we have noted, at first this conscious use of self will feel uncomfortable and unnatural. Practice makes it easier and with that practice comes the development of the counsellor's own style of working and behaving in the counselling relationship. No such style can develop if, first, the counsellor does not consciously consider the way she sits and the way she listens.

In summary, it is possible to identify some of those things that act as blocks to effective listening and some aids to effective listening. No doubt the reader can add to both of these lists and such additions will be useful in that they will be a reflection of your own strengths and limitations as a listener.

Blocks to effective listening

1. the counsellor's own problems
2. counsellor stress and anxiety
3. awkward/uncomfortable seating
4. lack of attention to listening behaviour
5. value judgements and interpretations on the part of the counsellor
6. the counsellor's attention focused in rather than out
7. rehearsals inside the counsellor's head

Aids to effective listening

1. attention focused out
2. suspension of judgement by the counsellor
3. attention to the behavioural aspects of listening
4. comfortable seating
5. avoidance of interpretation
6. development of free-floating attention
7. judicious use of minimal prompts

Listening in practice

David is a GP in a busy city-centre practice. He gets repeated visits from a young woman, Sarah, whose husband has recently been killed in a road accident. She often makes allusion to the problems of adjusting to her bereavement but presents with fairly minor physical ailments. David gently suggests to her that it may be helpful if they talked about her loss in more detail and offers her an after-noon appointment. At first she is reluctant to accept this but later

113

phones to make such an appointment. During the next few weeks, David meets Sarah on a regular basis and listens to her. During these appointments, he has to make very few verbal interventions: Sarah is able to describe and ventilate her feelings very easily once she is offered the opportunity. She works through stages of anger, extreme sorrow and meaninglessness and finally to some acceptance. During these stages, David has had to 'do' very little. His supportive attention and ability to listen, without making too many suggestions or offering too much advice has been therapeutic of itself. He realizes, however, that he has had to learn to listen. Previously in his career, he tended to finish a sentence for other people and has slowly learnt to focus attention upon the other person and really listen to him.

ATTENDING, LISTENING AND THE HEALTH PROFESSIONAL

The attending and listening aspects of counselling are essential skills that can be used in every health professional's job. The skills are clearly not limited only to use within the counselling relationship but can be applied in other interpersonal exchanges. An advantage of paying attention to the development of these particular skills is that becoming an effective listener not only makes for better counselling practice but interpersonal effectiveness and self-awareness are also enhanced. In the following chapters, verbal interventions are explored that will compliment the listening and attending described here. Again, such interventions can be used both inside and outside the counselling relationship and can do much to improve every health professional's performance as a carer.

7

Counselling skills II: client-centred skills

Counselling skills may be divided into two sub groups: (a) listening and attending and (b) counselling interventions. Listening and attending were considered in the previous chapter This chapter identifies important counselling interventions – the things that the counsellor says in the counselling relationship.

The term **client-centred**, first used by Carl Rogers (1951), refers to the notion that it is the client, himself, who is best able to decide how to find the solutions to his problems in living. Client-centred in this sense may be contrasted with the idea of counsellor-centred or professional-centred, both of which may suggest that someone other than the client is the expert. Whilst this may be true when applied to certain concrete factual problems: housing, surgery, legal problems and so forth, it is difficult to see how it can apply to issues in personal life. In such cases it is the client who identifies the problem and the client who, given time and space, can find their way through the problem to the solution.

Murgatroyd (1986) summarizes the client-centred position as follows:

1. A person in need has come to you for help;
2. In order to be helped they need to know that you have understood how they think and feel;
3. They also need to know that, whatever your own feelings about who or what they are or about what they have or have not done, you accept them as they are – you accept their right to decide their own lives for themselves;
4. In the light of this knowledge about your acceptance and understanding of them they will begin to open themselves to the possibility of change and development;

5. But if they feel that their association with you is conditional upon them changing, they may feel pressurized and reject your help.

The first issues identified by Murgatroyd, the fact of the client coming for help and needing to be understood and accepted, have been discussed in previous chapters. What we need to consider now are ways of helping the person to express himself, to open himself and thus to begin to change. It is worth noting, too, the almost paradoxical nature of Murgatroyd's last point: that if the client feels that his association with you is conditional upon him changing, he may reject your help. Thus, we enter into the counselling relationship without even being desirous of the other person changing!

In a sense, this is an impossible state of affairs. If we did not hope for change, presumably, we would not enter into the task of counselling in the first place! On another level, however, the point is a very important one. People change at their own rate and in their own time. The process cannot be rushed and we cannot will another person to change. Nor can we expect them to change to become more the sort of person that we would like them to be. We must meet them on their own terms and observe change as they wish and will it to be (or not, as the case may be). This sort of counselling, then, is a very altruistic sort. It demands of us that we make no demands of others.

Client-centred counselling is a **process** rather than a particular set of skills. It evolves through the relationship that the counsellor has with the client and vice versa. In a sense, it is a period of growth for both parties, for both learns from the other. It also involves the exercise of restraint. The counsellor must restrain herself from offering advice and from the temptation to put the client's life right for him. The outcome of such counselling cannot be predicted nor can concrete goals be set (unless they are devised by the client, at his request). In essence, client-centred counselling involves an act of faith: a belief in the other person's ability to find solutions through the process of therapeutic conversation and through the act of being engaged in a close relationship with another human being.

Certain basic, client-centred skills may be identified, although as we have noted, it is the total relationship that is important. Skills exercised in isolation amount to little: the warmth, genuineness and positive regard must also be present. On the other hand, if basic skills are not considered, then the counselling process will probably be shapeless or it will degenerate into the counsellor becoming prescriptive. The skill of standing back and allowing the client to find his own way is a difficult one to learn. The following skills may help in the process.

1. questions
2. reflection
3. selective reflection
4. empathy-building
5. checking for understanding

Each of these skills will now be considered in turn and in Chapter 11 a wide range of exercises is offered for the development of such skills. Each skill can be learned. In order for that to happen, each must be tried and practised. There is a temptation to say 'I do that anyway!' when reading a description of some of these skills. The point is to notice the doing of them and to practise doing them better! Whilst counselling often shares the characteristics of everyday conversation, if it is to progress beyond that it is important that some, if not all, of the following skills are used effectively, tactfully and skilfully.

QUESTIONS

Two main sorts of questions may be identified in the client-centred approach: closed and open questions.

Closed questions

A closed question is one that elicits a yes, a no or a similar one-word answer. Or it is one that the counsellor can anticipate an approximation of the answer, as she asks it. Examples of closed questions are as follows:

1. What is your name?
2. How many children do you have?
3. Are you happier now?
4. Are you still depressed?

Too many closed questions can make the counselling relationship seem like an interrogation! They also inhibit the development of the client's telling of his story and place the locus of responsibility in the relationship firmly with the client. Consider, for instance, the following exchange between marriage-guidance counsellor and client:

> *Counsellor:* Are you happier now. . . at home?
> *Client:* Yes, I think I am. . .
> *Counsellor:* Is that because you can talk more easily with your wife?
> *Client:* I think so. . . we seem to get on better, generally.
> *Counsellor:* And has your wife noticed the difference?
> *Client:* Yes, she has.

In this conversation, made up only of closed questions, the counsellor clearly leads the conversation. She also tends to try to influence the client towards accepting the idea that he is happier now and that his wife has noticed the difference. One of the problems with this sort of questioning is that it gives little opportunity for the client to disagree profoundly with the counsellor. In the previous exchange, for example, could the client easily have disagreed with the counsellor? It would seem not.

On the other hand, the closed question is useful in clarifying certain specific issues. For example, one may be used as follows:

> *Client:* It's not always easy at home. . . the children always seem to be so noisy. . . and my wife finds it difficult to cope with them.
> *Counsellor:* How many children have you?
> *Client:* Three. They're all under ten and they're at the sort of age when they use up a lot of energy and make a lot of noise.

Here, the closed question is fairly unobtrusive and serves to clarify the conversation. Notice, too, that once the question has been asked, the counsellor allows the client to continue to talk about his family, without further interruption.

Open questions

Open questions are those that do not elicit a particular answer: the counsellor cannot easily anticipate what an answer will 'look like'.

118

Examples of open questions include:

1. What did you do then?
2. How did you feel when that happened?
3. How are you feeling right now?
4. What do you think will happen?

Open questions are ones that encourage the client to say more, to expand on their story or to go deeper. An example of their use is as follows:

Counsellor: What is happening at home at the moment?
Client: Things are going quite well. Everyone's much more settled now and my son's found himself a job. He's been out of work for a long time.
Counsellor: How have you felt about that?
Client: It's upset me a lot. . . . It seemed wrong that I was working and he wasn't. . . he had to struggle for a long time. . . he wasn't happy at all.
Counsellor: And how are you feeling right now?
Client: Upset. . . I'm still upset. . . I still feel that I didn't help him enough.

In this conversation, the counsellor uses only open questions and the client expands on what he thinks and feels. More importantly, perhaps, this example illustrates the counsellor following the client and noting his paralinguistic and nonverbal cues. In this way, she is able to help the client to focus more on what is happening in the present. This is an example of the concreteness and immediacy referred to in Chapter 3.

Open questions are generally preferable, in counselling, to closed ones. They encourage longer, more expansive answers and are rather more free of value judgements and interpretation than are closed questions. All the same, the counsellor has to monitor the 'slope' of intervention when using open questions. It is easy, for example, to become intrusive by asking questions that are too piercing too quickly. As with all counselling interventions, the timing of the use of questions is vital.

When to use questions

Questions can be used in counselling relationships for a variety of purposes. The main ones include:

1. Exploration: What else happened? How did you feel then?
2. For further information: How many children have you got? What sort of work were you doing before you retired?
3. To clarify: I'm sorry, did you say you are going to move or did you say you're not sure? What did you say then?
4. Encouraging client-talk: Can you say more about that? What are your feelings about that?

Other sorts of questions

There are other ways of classifying questions and some to be avoided! Examples of other sorts of questions, include:

Leading questions

These are questions that contain an assumption that places the client in an untenable position. The classic example of a leading question is 'Have you stopped beating your wife?'! Clearly, however the question is answered, the client is in the wrong! Other examples of leading questions are: 'Is your depression the thing that's making your work so difficult? Are your family upset by your behaviour? Do you think that you may be hiding something. . . even from yourself?' The latter, pseudo-analytical questions are particularly awkward. What could the answer possibly be?

Value-laden questions

Questions such as 'Does your homosexuality make you feel guilty', not only possess a moral question but guarantees that the client feels difficult answering it!

'Why' questions

These have been discussed in Chapter 3 and the problems caused by them in the counselling relationship suggest that they should be used very sparingly, if at all.

Confronting questions

Examples of these may include: 'Can you give me an example of when that happened?' and 'Do you still love your wife?' Confrontation in counselling is quite appropriate once the relationship has fully developed but needs to be used skilfully and appropriately. It is easy for apparent confrontation to degenerate into moralizing. Heron (1986) and Schulman (1982) offer useful approaches to effective confrontation in counselling.

Funnelling

Funnelling (Kahn and Cannell, 1957) refers to the use of questions to guide the conversation from the general to the specific. Thus, the conversation starts with broad, opening questions and slowly, more specific questions are used to focus the discussion. An example of the use of funnelling is as follows:

> *Counsellor:* You seem upset at the moment, what's happening?
> *Client:* It's home. . . things aren't working out.
> *Counsellor:* What's happening at home?
> *Client:* I'm always falling out with Jane and the children.
> *Counsellor:* What does Jane feel about what's happening?
> *Client:* She's angry with me.
> *Counsellor:* About something in particular?
> *Client:* Yes, about the way I talk to Andrew, my son.
> *Counsellor:* What is the problem with Andrew?

In this way, the conversation becomes directed and focused and this may pose a problem. If the counsellor does use funnelling in this way, it is arguable that the counselling conversation is no longer client-centred but counsellor-directed. Perhaps, in many situations – particularly where shortage of time is an issue – a combination of following and leading may be appropriate. **Following** refers to the counsellor taking the lead from the client and exploring the avenues that he wants to explore. **Leading** refers to the counsellor taking a more active role and pursuing certain issues that she feels are important. If in doubt, however, the 'following' approach is probably preferable as it keeps the locus of control in the counselling relationship firmly with the client.

Funnelling in practice

Andy is a volunteer telephone counsellor on a local AIDS helpline. A young man of 18 rings in to ask about the symptoms of AIDS and for general information about the condition. Andy, in return, asks some open questions of the young man in order to establish a 'phone relationship'. As the conversation progresses, Andy gradually asks more specific questions and helps the young man to express more particular, personal anxieties about his own sexuality and his fear that he may be homosexual. Andy, through using the funnelling approach to the use of questions, is able to help the person through a difficult personal crisis that continues to be worked through in subsequent counselling sessions.

Reflection

Reflection (sometimes called **echoing**) is the process of reflecting back the last few words, or a paraphrase of the last few words, that the client has used in order to encourage him to say more. It is as though the counsellor is echoing the client's thoughts and as though that echo serves as a prompt. It is important that the reflection does not turn into a question and this is best achieved by the counsellor making the repetition in much the same tone of voice as the client used. An example of the use of reflection is as follows:

> *Client:* We had lived in the South for a number of years. Then we moved and I supposed that's when things started to go wrong.
> *Counsellor:* Things started to go wrong.
> *Client:* Well, we never really settled down. My wife missed her friends and I suppose I did really. . . though neither of us said anything.
> *Counsellor:* Neither of you said that you missed your friends.
> *Client:* We both tried to protect each other, really. I suppose if either of us had said anything, we would have felt that we were letting the other one down.

In this example, the reflections are unobtrusive and unnoticed by the client. They serve to help the client to say more, to develop his story. Used skilfully and with good timing, reflection can be an important method of helping the client. On the other hand, if it is overused or used clumsily, it can appear stilted and is very noticeable. Unfortunately, it is an intervention that takes some practice and one that many people anticipate learning on counselling courses. As a result, when people return from counselling courses, their friends and relatives are often waiting for them to use the technique and may comment on the fact! This should not be a deterrent as the method remains a useful and therapeutic one.

Selective reflection

Selective reflection refers to the method of repeating back to the client a part of something they said that was emphasized in some way or which seemed to be emotionally charged. Thus, selective reflection draws from the middle of the client's utterance and not from the end. An example of the use of selective reflection is as follows:

> *Client:* We had just got married. I was very young and I thought things would work out OK. We started buying our own house. My wife hated the place! It was important, though. . . we had to start somewhere.
> *Counsellor:* Your wife hated the house.
> *Client:* She thought it was the worst place she'd lived in! She reckoned that she would only live there for a year at the most and we ended up being there for five years!

The use of selective reflection allowed the client in this example to develop further an almost throwaway remark. Often, these asides are the substance of very important feelings and the counsellor can often help in the release of some of these feelings by using selective reflection to focus on them. Clearly concentration is important in order to note the points on which to selectively reflect. Also, the counselling relationship is a flowing, evolving conversation that tends to be 'seamless'. Thus, it is little use the counsellor storing up a point that she feels would be useful to selectively reflect! By the time a break comes in the conversation, the item will probably be irrelevant! This points up, again, the need to develop free-floating attention: the ability to allow the ebb and flow of the conversation to go where the client takes it and for the counsellor to trust her own ability to choose an appropriate intervention when a break occurs.

EMPATHY-BUILDING

This refers to the counsellor making statements to the client that indicate that she has understood the feeling that the client is experiencing. A certain intuitive ability is needed here, for often empathy-building statements refer more to what is implied than what is overtly said. An example of the use of such statements is as follows:

> *Client:* People at work are the same. They're all tied up with their own friends and families... they don't have a lot of time for me... though they're friendly enough.
> *Counsellor:* You sound angry with them.
> *Client:* I suppose I am! Why don't they take a bit of time to ask me how I'm getting on? It wouldn't take much!
> *Counsellor:* It sounds as though you are saying that people haven't had time for you for a long time.
> *Client:* They haven't. My family didn't bother much... I mean, they looked as though they did... but they didn't really.

The empathy-building statements, used here, are ones that read between the lines. Now sometimes, such reading between the lines can be completely wrong and the empathy-building statement is rejected by the client. It is important when this happens for the counsellor to drop the approach altogether and to pay more attention to listening. Inaccurate empathy-building statements often indicate an overwillingness on the part of the counsellor to become involved with the client's perceptual world – at the expense of accurate empathy! Used skilfully, however, they help the client to disclose further and indicate to the client that they are understood.

CHECKING FOR UNDERSTANDING

Checking for understanding involves either (a) asking the client if you have understood them correctly or (b) occasionally summarizing the conversation in order to clarify what has been said. The first type of checking is useful when the client quickly covers a lot of topics and seems to be thinking aloud. It can be used to focus the conversation further or as a means of ensuring that the counsellor really stays with what the client is saying. The second type of checking should be used sparingly or the counselling conversation can seem to get rather mechanical and studied. The following two examples illustrate the two uses of checking for understanding.

Example one

> *Client:* I feel all over the place at the moment... things aren't quite right at work... money is still a problem and I don't seem to be talking to anyone... I'm not sure about work... sometimes I feel like packing it in... at other times I think I'm doing OK.
>
> *Counsellor:* Let me just clarify... you're saying things are generally a problem at the moment and you've thought about leaving work?
>
> *Client:* Yes... I don't think I will stop work but if I can get to talk it over with my boss, I think I will feel easier about it.

Example two

> *Counsellor:* Let me see if I can just sum up what we've talked about this afternoon. We talked about the financial problems and the question of talking to the bank manager. You suggested that you may ask him for a loan. Then you went on to say how you felt you could organize your finances better in the future.
>
> *Client:* Yes, I think that covers most things.

Some counsellors prefer to use the second type of checking at the end of each counselling session and this may help to clarify things before the client leaves. On the other hand, there is much to be said for not tidying up the end of the session in this way. If the loose ends are left, the client continues to think about all the issues that have been discussed as he walks away from the session. If everything is summarized too neatly, the client may feel that the problems can be 'closed down' for a while or even worse, that they have been solved! Personal problems are rarely simple enough to be summarized in a few words and the uses of checking at the end of a session should be used sparingly.

These, then, are particular skills that encourage self-direction on the part of the client and can be learned and used by the counsellor. They form the basis of all good counselling and can always be

125

returned to as a primary way of working with the client in the counselling relationship.

The client-centred approach in practice

Mary, a health visitor, is asked by one of her young single-parent clients about her young daughter's inability to sleep. Mary uses client-centred interventions and draws out the details surrounding the family situation. In allowing the young mother to talk through her financial and emotional worries, she allows some of the pressure on the mother to be dispelled. She follows this up with some practical suggestions about how to help the daughter to sleep, including the suggestions of a regular bedtime, a planned routine during the evening and a 'winding-down' period before going to bed. The combination of allowing the mother to talk out her own anxieties and offering practical suggestions enable both mother and daughter to live more comfortably.

CLIENT-CENTRED SKILLS AND THE HEALTH PROFESSIONAL

Whilst the discussion, in this chapter, has focused on the use of client-centred interventions in the counselling relationship, the range of skills involved is clearly useful in a wide range of health contexts. Workers in the primary health-care team may use them as part of their assessment programme whilst professionals in longer term care can use them as supportive measures and as a means of evaluating the effectiveness of care. In nursing, they may be used to draw up care plans and to implement, effectively, the use of nursing models – particularly self-care models. In the next chapter, consideration will be made of how to combine these client-centred interventions with those that help clients to express and handle emotions and feelings.

8

Counselling skills III:
helping with feelings

A considerable part of the process of helping people in counselling is concerned with the emotional or 'feelings' side of the person. In the UK and North American cultures, a great premium is placed on the individual's being able to control feelings and thus overt expression of emotion is often frowned upon. As a result, we learn to bottle up feelings, sometimes from a very early age. In this chapter, we will consider the effects of such suppression of feelings and identify some practical ways of helping people to identify and explore their feelings. The skills involved in managing feelings can be seen to augment the skills discussed in the previous chapter – the basic client-centred counselling skills.

TYPES OF EMOTION

Heron (1977a) distinguishes between at least four types of emotion that are commonly suppressed or bottled up: anger, fear, grief and embarrassment. He notes a relationship between these feelings and certain overt expressions of them. Thus, in counselling, anger may be expressed as loud sound, fear as trembling, grief through tears and embarrassment by laughter. He notes, also, a relationship between those feelings and certain basic human needs. Heron argues that we all have the need to understand and know what is happening to us. If that knowledge is not forthcoming, we may experience fear. We need, also, to make choices in our lives and if that choice is restricted in certain ways, we may feel anger. Thirdly, we need to experience the expression of love and of being loved. If that love is denied us or taken away from us, we may experience grief. To Heron's basic human needs may be added the need for self-respect and dignity. If such dignity is denied us, we may feel self-conscious and embarrassed. Practical examples of how these relationships work in everyday life and in the counselling relationship may be illustrated as follows:

Example one

A 20-year-old girl is attempting to live in a flat on her own. Her parents, however, insist on visiting her regularly and making suggestions as to how she should decorate the flat. They also regularly buy her articles for it and gradually she senses that she is feeling very uncomfortable and distanced from her parents. In the counselling relationship she discovers that she is very angry: her desire to make choices for herself is continually being eroded by her parents' benevolence.

Example two

A 45-year-old man hears that his mother is seriously ill and subsequently, she dies. He feels no emotions except that of feeling 'frozen' and unemotional. During a counselling session he suddenly discovers the need to cry profoundly. As he does so, he realizes that, many years ago, he had decided that crying was not a masculine thing to do. As a result, he blocked off his grief and felt numb, until, within the safety of the counselling relationship, he was able to discover his grief and express it.

Example three

An 18-year-old boy, discussing his college work, during a counselling sessions begins to laugh almost uncontrollably. As he does so, he begins to feel the laughter turning to tears. Through his mixed laughter and tears he acknowledges that 'No-one ever took me seriously... not at school, at home... or anywhere'. His laughter may be an expression of his lack of self-esteem and his tears, the grief he experiences at that lack.

In the third example it may be noted how emotions that are suppressed are rarely only of one sort. Very often, bottled-up emotion is a mixture of anger, fear, embarrassment and grief. Often, too, the causes of such blocked emotion are unclear and lost in the history of the person. What is perhaps more important is that the expression of pent-up emotion is often helpful in that it seems to allow the person to be clearer in his thinking once he has expressed it. It is as though the blocked emotion 'gets in the way' and its release acts as a means of helping the person to clarify his thoughts and feelings. It is notable that the suppression of feelings can lead to certain problems in living that may be clearly identified.

THE EFFECTS OF BOTTLING UP EMOTION

Physical discomfort and muscular pain

Wilhelm Reich, a psychoanalyst with a particular interest in the relationship between emotions and the musculature noted that blocked emotions could become trapped in the body's muscle clusters (Reich, 1949). Thus, he noted that anger was frequently 'trapped' in the muscles of the shoulders, grief in muscles surrounding the stomach and fear in the leg muscles. Often, these trapped emotions lead to chronic postural problems. Sometimes, the thorough release of the blocked emotion can lead to a freeing up of the muscles and an improved physical appearance. Reich believed in working directly on the muscle clusters in order to bring about emotional release and subsequent freedom from suppression and out of his work was developed a particular type of mind–body therapy, known as **bioenergetics** (Lowen, 1967; Lowen and Lowen, 1977).

In terms of everyday counselling, trapped emotion is sometimes visible in the way that the client holds himself and the skilled counsellor can learn to notice tension in the musculature and changes in breathing patterns that may suggest muscular tension. We have noted throughout this book how difficult it is to interpret another person's behaviour. What is important, here, is that such bodily manifestations be used only as a clue to what may be happening in the person. We cannot assume that a person who looks tense is tense, until he has said that he is.

Health professionals will be very familiar with the link between body posture, the musculature and the emotional state of the person. Frequently, if patients and clients can be helped to relax, then their medical and psychological condition may improve more quickly. Those health professionals who deal most directly with the muscle clusters (remedial gymnasts and physiotherapists, for example) will tend to notice physical tension more readily but all carers can train themselves to observe these important indicators of the emotional status of the person in their care.

Difficulty in decision-making

This is a frequent side effect of bottled-up emotion. It is as though the emotion makes the person uneasy and that uneasiness leads to lack of confidence. As a result, that person finds it difficult to rely on his own resources and may find decision-making difficult. When we are under stress of any sort it is often the case that we feel the need to check decisions with other people. Once some of this stress is removed by talking through problems or by releasing pent-up emotions, the decision-making process often becomes easier.

Faulty self-image

When we bottle up feelings, those feelings often have an unpleasant habit of turning against us. Thus, instead of expressing anger towards others, we turn it against ourselves and feel depressed as a result. Or, if we have hung onto unexpressed grief, we turn that grief in on ourselves and experience ourselves as less than we are. Often in counselling, as old resentments or dissatisfactions are expressed, so the person begins to feel better about himself.

Setting unrealistic goals

Tension can lead to further tension. This tension can lead us to set ourselves unreachable goals. It is almost as though we set ourselves up to fail! Sometimes, too, failing is a way of punishing ourselves or it is safer than achieving. Release of tension through the expression of emotion can sometimes help a person to take a more realistic view of himself and his goal-setting.

The development of long-term faulty beliefs

Sometimes emotion that has been bottled up for a long time can lead to a person's view of the world being coloured in a particular way. He learns that people can't be trusted or that people always let you down in the end. It is as though old, painful feelings lead to distortions that become part of that person's world view. Such long-term distorted beliefs about the world do not change easily but may be modified as the person comes to release feelings and learns to handle his emotions more effectively.

130

The 'last straw' syndrome

Sometimes, if emotion is bottled up for a considerable amount of time, a valve blows and the person hits out – either literally or verbally. We have all experienced the problem of storing up anger and taking it out on someone else, a process that is sometimes called **displacement**. The original object of our anger is now replaced by something or someone else. Again, the talking through of difficulties or the release of pent-up emotion can often help to ensure that the person does not feel the need to explode in this way.

Clearly, no two people react to the bottling up of emotion in the same way. Some people, too, choose not to deal with life events emotionally. It would be curious to argue that there is a norm where emotions are concerned. On the other hand, many people complain of being unable to cope with emotions and if the client perceives that there is a problem in the emotional domain, then that perception may be expressed as a desire to explore his emotional status. It is important, however, that the counsellor does not force her particular set of beliefs about feelings and emotions on the client, but waits to be asked to help. Often the request for such help is a tacit request: the client talks about difficulty in dealing with emotion and that in itself may safely be taken as a request for help. A variety of methods is available to the counsellor to help in the exploration of the domain of feelings and those methods will be described. Sometimes, these methods produce **catharsis** – the expression of strong emotion – tears, anger, fear, laughter. Drawing on the literature on the subject, the following statements may be made about the handling of such emotional release:

1. Emotional release is usually self-limiting. If the person is allowed to cry or get angry, that emotion will be expressed and will then gradually subside. The supportive counsellor will allow it to happen and not become unduly distressed by it.
2. Physical support can sometimes be helpful in the form of holding the person's hand or putting an arm round them. Care should be taken, however, that such actions are unambiguous and that the holding of the client is not too tight. A very tight embrace is likely to inhibit the release of emotion. It is worth remembering, also, that not everyone likes or wants physical contact. It is important that the counsellor's support is not seen as intrusive by the client.
3. Once the person has had a cathartic release they will need time

to piece together the insights that they gain from such release. Often all that is needed is that the counsellor sits quietly with the client while he occasionally verbalizes what he is thinking. The post-cathartic period can be a very important stage in the counselling process.

4. There seems to be a link between the amount we can allow another person to express emotion and the degree to which we can handle our own emotion. This is another reason why the counsellor needs self-awareness. To help others explore their feelings we need, first, to explore our own. Many colleges and university departments offer workshops on cathartic work and self-awareness development that can help in both training the counsellor to help others and in gaining self-insight.

5. Frequent cathartic counselling can be exhausting for the counsellor and if she is to avoid burnout, she needs to set up a network of support from other colleagues or via a peer-support group. We cannot hope to handle other people's emotional release constantly, without its taking a toll on us.

METHODS OF HELPING THE CLIENT TO EXPLORE FEELINGS

These are practical methods that can be used in the counselling relationship to help the client to identify, examine and, if required, release emotion. Most of them will be more effective if the counsellor has first tried them on herself. This can be done simply by reading through the description of them and then trying them out, in one's mind. Alternatively, they can be tried out with a colleague or friend. Another way of exploring their effectiveness is to use them in a peer-support context. The setting up and running of such a group is described in the final chapter of this book, along with various exercises that can be used to improve counselling skills. All of the following activities should be used gently and thoughtfully and timed to fit in with the client's requirements. There should never be any sense of pushing the client to explore feelings because of a misplaced belief that 'a good cry will do him good!'

Giving permission

Sometimes in counselling, the client tries desperately to hang on to strong feelings and not to express them. As we have seen, this may be due to the cultural norm that suggests that holding on is often better than letting go. Thus, a primary method for helping someone to explore his emotions is for the counsellor to 'give permission' for the expression of feeling. This can be done simply through acknowledging that 'It's alright with me if you feel you are going to cry'. In this way the counsellor has reassured the client that expression of feelings is acceptable within the relationship. Clearly, a degree of tact is required here. It is important that the client does not feel pushed into expressing feelings that he would rather not express. The permission-giving should never be coercive nor should there be an implicit suggestion that 'you must express your feelings!'

Literal description

This refers to inviting the client to think back in time about a place that he has, until now, only alluded to and to ask him to describe that place in some detail. An example of this use of literal description is as follows:

> *Client:* I used to get like this at home. . . I used to get very upset.
> *Counsellor:* Just go back home for a moment. . . describe one of the rooms in the house.
> *Client:* The front room faces directly out onto the street. . . there is an armchair by the window. . . the TV in the corner. . . our dog is lying on the rug. . . it's very quiet.
> *Counsellor:* What are your feelings right now?
> *Client:* Like I was then. . . angry. . . upset.

Going back to and describing in literal terms a place that was the scene of an emotional experience can often bring that emotion back. When the counsellor has invited the client to literally describe a particular place, she then asks him to identify the feeling that emerges from that description. It is important that the description has an 'I am there' quality about it and does not slip into a detached description such as 'We lived in a big house which wasn't particularly modern but then my parents didn't like modern houses much'.

Locating and developing a feeling in terms of the body

As we have noted on p. 129, very often feelings are accompanied by a physical sensation. It is often helpful to identify that physical experience and to invite the client to exaggerate it, to allow the feeling to expand in order to explore it further. An example of this approach is as follows:

Counsellor: How are you feeling at the moment?
Client: Slightly anxious.
Counsellor: Where, in terms of your body, do you feel the anxiety?
Client: (rubs stomach) Here.
Counsellor: Can you increase that feeling in your stomach?
Client: Yes, it's spreading up to my chest.
Counsellor: And what's happening now?
Client: It reminds me of a long time ago. . . when I first started work.
Counsellor: What happened there?

Again, the original suggestion by the counsellor is followed through by a question to elicit how the client is feeling following the suggestion. This gives the client a chance to identify the thoughts that go with that feeling and to explore them further.

The empty chair

Another method of exploring feelings is to invite the client to imagine the feeling that they are experiencing as sitting in a chair next to them and then to have them address the feeling. This can be used in a variety of ways and the next examples show its applications:

Example one

Client: I feel very confused at the moment, I can't seem to sort things out.
Counsellor: Can you imagine your confusion sitting in that chair over there. . . what does it look like?
Client: It looks like a great big ball of wool. . . how odd!
Counsellor: If you could speak to your confusion, what would you say to it?

Client: I wish I could sort you out!

Counsellor: And what's your confusion saying back to you?

Client: I'm glad you don't sort me out – I stop you from having to make any decisions!

Counsellor: And what do you make of that?

Client: I suppose that could be true... the longer I stay confused, the less I have to make decisions about my family.

Example two

Counsellor: How are you feeling about the people you work with? You said you found it quite difficult to get on with them.

Client: Yes, it's still difficult, especially my boss.

Counsellor: Imagine your boss is sitting in that chair over there. How does that feel?

Client: Uncomfortable! He's angry with me!

Counsellor: What would you like to say to him?

Client: Why do I always feel scared of you... why do you make me feel uncomfortable?

Counsellor: And what does he say?

Client: I don't! It's you that feels uncomfortable, not me... You make yourself uncomfortable. (To the counsellor) He's right! I do make myself uncomfortable but I use him as an excuse.

The empty chair can be used in a variety of ways to set up a dialogue between either the client and his feelings or between the client and a person that the client talks about. It offers a very direct way of exploring relationships and feelings and deals directly with the issue of **projection**: the tendency we have to see qualities in others that are, in fact, our own. Using the empty-chair technique can bring to light those projections and allow the client to see them for what they are. Other applications of this method are described in detail by Perls (1969).

Contradiction

It is sometimes helpful if the client is asked to contradict a statement that they make, especially when that statement contains some ambiguity. An example of this approach is as follows:

Client: (looking at the floor) I've sorted everything out now. Everything's OK.

Counsellor: Try contradicting what you've just said.

Client: Everything's not OK. Everything isn't sorted out (laughs). That's true, of course, there's a lot more to sort out yet.

Mobilization of body energy

Developing the theme discussed on p. 129 regarding the idea that emotions can be trapped within the body's musculature, it is sometimes helpful for the counsellor to suggest to the client that he stretches, or takes some very deep breaths. In the process, the client may become aware of tensions that are trapped in his body and may begin to recognize and identify those tensions. This, in turn, can lead to the client talking about and expressing some of those tensions. This is particularly helpful if, during the counselling conversation, the client becomes less and less mobile and adopts a particularly hunched or curled-up position in his chair. The invitation to stretch serves almost as a contradiction to the body position being adopted by the client at that time.

Exploring fantasy

We often set fairly arbitrary limits on what we think we can and cannot do. When a client seems to be doing this, it is sometimes helpful to explore what may happen if this limit was broken. An example of this is as follows:

Client: I'd like to be able to go abroad for a change, I never seem to go very far on holiday.

Counsellor: What stops you?

Client: Flying, I suppose.

Counsellor: What's the worst thing about flying?

Client: I get very anxious.

Counsellor: And what happens if you get very anxious?

Client: Nothing really. I just get anxious.

Counsellor: So nothing terrible can happen if you allow yourself to get anxious?

Client: No, not really. . . I hadn't thought about it like that before.

Rehearsal

Sometimes the anticipation of a coming event or situation is anxiety-provoking. The counsellor can usefully help the client to explore a range of feelings by rehearsing a future event with him. Thus, the client who is anticipating a forthcoming interview may be helped by having the counsellor act the role of an interviewer, with a subsequent discussion afterwards. The client who wants to develop the assertive behaviour to enable him to challenge his boss may benefit from role-playing the situation in the counselling session. In each case it is important that both client and counsellor get into role and that the session does not just become a discussion of what may or may not happen. The actual playing through and rehearsal of a situation is nearly always more powerful than a discussion of it. Alberti and Emmons (1982) offer some useful suggestions about how to set up role-plays and exercises for developing assertive behaviour and Wilkinson and Canter (1982) describe some useful approaches to developing socially skilled behaviour. Often, if the client can practice effective behaviour, then the appropriate thoughts and feelings can accompany that behaviour. The novelist, Kurt Vonnegut, wryly commented that: 'We are what we pretend to be – so take care what you pretend to be' (Vonnegut, 1968). Sometimes, the first stage in changing is trying out a new pattern of behaviour or a new way of thinking and feeling. Practice, therefore, is invaluable.

This approach develops from the idea that what we think influences what we feel and do. If our thinking is restrictive, we may begin to feel that we can or cannot do certain things. Sometimes having these barriers to feeling and doing challenged can free a person to think, feel and act differently.

These methods of exploring feelings can be used alongside the client-centred interventions described in the previous chapter. They need to be practised in order that the counsellor feels confident in using them and the means to developing the skills involved are identified in the final chapter of this book. The domain of feelings is one that is frequently addressed in counselling. Counselling people who want to explore feelings takes time and cannot be rushed. Also, the development and use of the various skills described here is not the whole of the issue. Health professionals working with emotions need, also, to have developed the personal qualities that have been described elsewhere: warmth, genuineness, empathic understanding and unconditional positive regard. Emotional counselling can never be a mechanical process but is one that touches the lives of both client and counsellor.

Helping with feelings in practice: I

Jane is a student nurse on a busy medical ward. She develops a close relationship with Arthur Davis, an elderly man who has been treated for heart failure. Suddenly and unexpectedly, Mr Davis dies. Jane finds herself unable to come to terms with this and seeks the help of an older tutor in the school of nursing. The tutor helps her to talk through her feelings and she cries a great deal. Through the process of talking and crying she comes to realize that Arthur Davis reminded her of her own father, who had also died suddenly and for whom she had been unable to grieve. In grieving for Mr Davis, she was enabled to work through some of her grief for her own father.

Helping with feelings in practice: II

Andrew is a radiographer in a large accident and emergency department. He has recently had difficulties in his marriage that he feels affect his work in the department. He is able to talk this through with his superintendent, who has had training as a counsellor. During the course of the conversation, Andrew feels close to tears. His superintendent says: 'What would happen if you allowed yourself to cry?' Andrew smiles wryly and says 'Nothing'. With that, he bursts into tears and is allowed to cry. Afterwards, he finds it much easier to talk through his problems in a rational and systematic way and feels able to make more sense of what is happening at home. The superintendent's skilful and well-timed intervention allows Andrew the prompt that he needed to enable him to express bottled-up feelings.

HELPING WITH FEELINGS AND THE HEALTH PROFESSIONAL

As with other counselling interventions, the ones that deal with the expression of feelings have a wider application than just the counselling relationship. There are many occasions in the health-care world in which the professional is called upon to help and support the person who is in emotional distress. Sometimes, such situations arise as something of an emergency or arise suddenly and without warning. The professional who has considered the skills involved in helping with the expression of emotion is likely to be better equipped to deal with these emergencies when they arise.

9

Problems and support in counselling

Counselling takes time and energy on the part of the counsellor. The fact of being intimately involved in someone else's world means that both counsellor and client form a close and sometimes painful relationship. If counselling is to be successful, it will involve change on the part of the client. It may also involve change on the part of the counsellor. Now most of us resist change – we prefer to stay as we are. In counselling it often seems as though the client wants problem resolution without having to change himself! Clearly, life problems cannot change without the person who experiences them changing too. The nature of the counselling relationship, then, is one that develops, regresses, modulates and is finally outgrown. Along that dimension, various difficulties can arise and in this chapter a number of such problems are identified and explored.

TRANSFERENCE AND COUNTERTRANSFERENCE

As the client discloses himself to the counsellor, so an element of dependence creeps into the relationship. Because the counsellor is accepting what the client has to say, the client may begin to cast the counsellor in the role of a person from the past who has also adopted this accepting, allowing position – a trusted parent. Transference refers to the client's coming to view the counsellor as if they were the all-forgiving, positive parent. The net result of this perception is that the client may come to view the counsellor as having exceptionally positive qualities: the client may temporarily come to view the counsellor as one of the most important people in his life.

Countertransference, on the other hand, refers to the feelings that the counsellor develops for the client. Usually, too, these are positive in nature and fed by the positive feelings that the client expresses for the counsellor. A problem arises, however, if the counsellor does not notice that she is being cast in the good-parent role and begins to unawarely play mother (or father) to the client's son (or daughter). What happens, then, is that old child/parent relationships are played out by the client with the counsellor and little progression is achieved. The counsellor unconsciously concludes with the role that the client has cast her in and the relationship staggers on until either the client finds little reward in it, discovers that the counsellor is only human after all, or the counsellor finds the whole relationship too claustrophobic and releases herself from the relationship.

Two practical approaches may be taken to the question of transference and countertransference. One is that the counsellor learns to notice what happens as the relationship develops and looks out for growing dependence on the part of the client. As the dependence develops, the counsellor can encourage the client, also, to become aware of it and make the counselling relationship itself the subject of discussion. Thus a joint focus is maintained in the counselling sessions – the client's life problems and the counsellor/client relationship. Much can be learned from the latter that will help with the former, for the quality of the client–counsellor relationship can do much to inform both parties and other relationships the client may have. It is as though the client–counsellor relationship represents one intense example of how the client relates to other people in everyday life.

The second approach to dealing with transference and counter-transference is for the counsellor to consider having an experienced colleague to act as supervisor during the counselling relationship. The supervisor serves as a person with whom the counselling relationship can be discussed confidentially and who may offer suggestions as to how she sees the counselling developing. Thus another, arguably objective, point of view is offered that may enable the counsellor to gain a little more objectivity herself. Three types of contract may usefully be used in the counsellor–supervisor relationship:

1. The supervisor agrees only to listen to the counsellor talking through her difficulties in the counselling relationship;
2. The supervisor agrees to make occasional comments as the counsellor talks;
3. The supervisor agrees to make intensive interventions during the

conversation and may act in the capacity of 'devil's advocate' to explore in detail the relationship that the counsellor has built up with the client.

These three contracts, agreed at the beginning of the counsellor–supervisor relationship can serve to determine the degree of involvement that the supervisor has. Obviously and at any time, the contract can be changed to meet the altering needs of the counsellor.

Through regular meetings with a supervisor, the counsellor can work through the sometimes painful period of the counsellor–client relationship in which transference is at its most acute.

Another basis for meetings between counsellor and supervisor is for the counsellor to write out the counsellor–client dialogue after the counselling session, as she remembers it. This then serves as a basis for discussions between counsellor and supervisor and can also help in identifying the counsellor's growing skill in using counselling interventions effectively.

The supervisor's role in the relationship is not as counselling expert but as one who listens and perhaps offers her perception of what is going on between counsellor and client. No counsellor gets to the point where they do not need a supervisor. The support offered by such a person is useful to the health practitioner who is just beginning a counselling role and also to the expert who has had many years experience.

Transference in practice

Geoff is an occupational therapist (OT) in a unit aiming to rehabilitate those with long-term psychiatric illnesses, in a large psychiatric hospital. He is trying to encourage the development of effective social skills with a small group of five patients and organizes role-modelling, practice and reinforcement of socially acceptable behaviour. He finds one younger patient very difficult to cope with and begins to feel that he does not like that patient. He allows the situation to continue for some time but finds himself becoming increasingly hostile towards the young man. Finally, Geoff is able to talk through his feelings with the Head OT, with whom he has a good relationship. The latter, who has had counselling training is able to explore with Geoff what it is that makes the young patient so unacceptable to him. During the course of their conversations, it becomes apparent that the young man reminds Geoff partly of himself as a younger person and partly of his younger brother, with whom he had never got on. The identification of this transference relationship allows Geoff to explore ways in which the young patient is different to both Geoff and his brother. In this way, Geoff becomes able to 'disidentify' with the associations he has made and to see the patient more clearly for his own strengths and weaknesses. Geoff is able to return to the social-skills group and work with the young man in a more constructive way.

DEALING WITH BLOCKS IN COUNSELLING

Periodically in many counselling relationships, a point may be reached where the client appears to be making little progress and the relationship seems to be stuck. At least two practical approaches may be taken to this problem. First, the counsellor can acknowledge to the client that she perceives the relationship to be stuck and thus verbalizes and makes explicit what has previously only been hinted at. This, in itself, can serve to push the relationship on and can open up discussion on other things that are not being talked about. Sometimes the block is caused, unknowingly, by the counsellor herself. If the client is discussing a problem that is also a problem for the counsellor, then the counsellor may skirt round the issue unawares rather than face it. Few of us like our own, unresolved problems brought out into the open, particularly by someone else! This highlights, further, the need for the prospective counsellor to develop self-awareness and to explore some of her own life problems before helping others to tackle theirs.

A second approach to dealing with blocks in the counselling relationship is to allow or even encourage the block to remain unresolved. This paradoxical way of working can sometimes be particularly effective. It is as though if we allow the problem to exist, then problem resolution is encouraged. On the other hand, the more we fight blocks, the more they continue to be a problem. The facing up to, accepting and staying with the block can be a productive means of allowing the relationship to develop. Sometimes, the longer we can stay confused about where the relationship is going, the more successful the outcome.

COPING WITH SILENCE

There are many occasions on which the counselling relationship falls into silence. So, too, there are different sorts of silences, from the meditative, thoughtful silence through to the hostile, angry silence. One thing is important, here: that the counsellor learns to differentiate between the sort of silence in which a counsellor intervention is called for and the sort of silence in which the client is quietly thinking things through. Normally, when the client is asking for the counsellor to say something, he will make eye contact with her and look towards her. When he is thinking about things, his eyes will usually be defocused or, sometimes, looking upwards (Bandler and Grinder, 1982). It is important that, because of anxiety about the silence, the counsellor does not overtalk. It is tempting to imagine that every silence needs filling and if the client isn't talking, then the counsellor should! Thoughtful silences are often some of the most productive aspects of counselling. Occasionally, too, however, it is helpful for the counsellor to ask, 'What are you thinking?' or 'What's the thought?'. These are particularly useful when the client suddenly falls silent, or stops his train of conversation and glances to one side. Often these are indicators of sudden insight that may (or may not) be usefully verbalized.

CONFRONTATION IN COUNSELLING

There are times when the counselling relationship can be purely client-centred. There are occasions on which the counsellor needs to draw attention to particular behaviours or beliefs that are negatively affecting the client's life. There are times, too, when we have to confront the client with bad news – news of a sudden death, for example. At other times, still, we need to be able to tell the client of the effect they are having on us.

The prospect of confrontation often causes anxiety. Two classic ways of reacting to that anxiety in the counsellor are outlined by Heron, 1986 in Figure 9.1. He describes two extremes: the 'pussyfooting' approach, where the counsellor skirts gently all round the topic but never comes to the point and the 'sledgehammer' approach, where the counsellor allows her anxiety about confrontation to build up to the point were it is all blurted out in one go and may degenerate to the point where a verbal attack is made on the client. This, perhaps, is a version of the 'last straw' syndrome, described on p. 131. Neither approach is very effective. A more constructive approach is the assertive, confronting approach in which the counsellor clearly and quietly states what it is she wants to

Figure 9.1 Confrontation and its variants.

---

1. **'Pussyfooting' approach:** the counsellor is vague, unclear and has a tendency to 'go round the houses';

2. **'Sledgehammer' approach:** the counsellor becomes aggressive and interventions become an attack on the person;

3. **Confronting approach:** the counsellor stays calm, keeps to the point and is prepared to repeat her confronting statement.

---

confront the client on and remains ready, if necessary, to repeat the confrontation. Such repetition may be necessary because there can be no guarantee how the client will react to clear, assertive confrontation. Some people respond by becoming submissive and quiet. The temptation, here, may be to 'back off' and to withdraw the confrontation. On the other hand, some people respond by becoming angry and again (though for different reasons) the counsellor may feel tempted to withdraw. The most effective approach, however, would seem to be to stay with the confrontation and to ensure that it is heard. A note of caution needs to be sounded, however, in that it is easy for the counsellor to overtalk in these situations and to overstate the confrontation because of the anxiety generated by the task. Effective confrontation usually involves the confrontation being made and then allowing time for it to sink in.

Another approach to confrontation is the **sandwich** approach. Three stages are involved in this method. In the first stage (or the 'top slice of the sandwich'), warning of the confrontation is given by the counsellor to the client. This is immediately followed up by the confrontation itself (the 'filling of the sandwich'). The third stage involves the counsellor offering the client support, without withdrawing the confrontation in any way (the 'bottom layer of the sandwich'). An example of this in action is as follows, where the counsellor has to give the client news of a relative's death.

Counsellor: I have some very bad news for you. I'm sorry to tell you that your mother died earlier this afternoon. I know it will be a great shock to you and I want you to know that I will stay with you.

What are the principles behind the sandwich approach? First, the warning that comes before the confrontation allows the client to anticipate the coming confrontation. It is important, however, that the confronting statement follows almost immediately, so that the client does not have to imagine, for too long, what form the confrontation will take. The final layer of the sandwich offers the client some means of support after experiencing the confrontation. Notice that in this offering of very bad news, the language used is completely unambiguous. It is vital when breaking bad news that there can be no doubt as to the meaning of the confrontation. Thus, all euphemisms should be avoided for the sake of clarity.

The sandwich approach in action

Joe is a social worker with a case load that covers a large housing estate. He is asked by his director to follow up a report that has been sent in by a local schoolteacher that suggests that one of the children in her class may have received nonaccidental injuries in the home. Joe visits the child's house and meets his parents. His first task is to develop rapport with the parents and he does this by introducing himself and by discussing his role and by then discretely asking the parents about themselves. He follows this, directly, by suggesting that he has some difficult issues to talk about and moves straight into outlining what those issues are. He then offers the parents the chance to talk things through in detail, to establish their reactions to the accusations. He then 'backs off' and allows the parents to react to the report, having used the 'sandwich' method of breaking difficult and upsetting news to the parents.

Example of a confrontation approach

This approach can be used in a variety of confronting contexts. Examples of the sorts of situations in which the counsellor may be required to confront the client may be enumerated as follows:

1. When the counsellor has to give the client difficult or shocking information (e.g. the death of a relative, notice of a diagnosis or challenging in suspected cases of child abuse);
2. When the client is using compulsive, negative self-statements (e.g. 'I'll never be able to walk again... I've never been any good at anything');
3. When the client is using 'games' in the relationship and

manipulating the counsellor (e.g. the 'Yes, but' game, where the client answers every suggestion the counsellor makes with the phrase 'Yes, I would, but. . .' (For further details of this sort of game playing, see Berne, 1964; James and Jongeward, 1971; Harris, 1973).

4. When contractual issues need to be clarified (e.g. previously agreed times of meeting and of finishing the counselling sessions);

5. When excuses need to be challenged. Wheeler and Janis (1980) identifying the following sorts of excuses that a client may use:
   (a) complacency: the 'it won't happen to me' attitude
   (b) rationalization: the 'it's not as bad as it looks' approach
   (c) procrastination: the 'nothing needs to be done at the moment' approach
   (d) passing the buck: the 'I'm not the one who needs to do something' idea

Arguably, all of these excuses may have to be confronted at various stages in certain counselling relationships. Care needs to be taken, however, that counselling of this sort does not degenerate into heavy-handed patronage of the client by the counsellor.

Of all the aspects of counselling, perhaps effective confrontation is the most difficult and needs the most practice. It is worth reflecting on how *you* handle confrontation!

Confrontation in practice

Julia is a speech therapist working with a young child, Clare, who has hearing problems. During one of their appointments, Clare's mother begins to tell Julia of Clare's difficult behaviour at home and is very critical of the child. She does this with the child sitting in front of both Julia and her mother. Julia reaches out and gently holds the mother's arm and says, 'I would appreciate it if we could talk about this in a few minutes when Clare goes in to see the doctor'. The mother, however, continues to talk negatively about her daughter. Julia repeats: 'I want to stop you and suggest that we talk in a few minutes'. After a third repetition of the request by Julia, Clare's mother stops talking but is encouraged to talk more freely when her daughter is not present. At a later appointment, Julia, Clare and her mother are more easily able to talk freely between themselves. Clare's mother has been able to 'offload' to Julia, without hurting her daughter's feelings. In the instance described here, Julia has confronted the mother and used the **broken record** method to ensure that what she wanted to say got through. This method refers to the technique of repeating, calmly, the confronting statement, until it is 'heard'.

THE LIMITS OF COUNSELLING

Much of the counselling that health professionals will be involved in will concern what may be called the 'worried well': people who have particular life problems but who are essentially mentally well. Whilst the question of where 'wellness' ends and mental illness begins is by no means clear cut, the health professional should always bear in mind her limitations. It is tempting, once we have established a close relationship with another person, to believe that we alone can help them. Sometimes it is with extreme reluctance that we call in other advice or help. It is, however, important that we only take on relationships that we can handle and in which we can be therapeutic. Clients who may present problems that the health professional working as counsellor may not be able to help, adequately include:

1. the person who is clinically depressed and talking of suicide
2. the person who is hallucinated or deluded
3. the person who has an organic mental illness
4. the person whose behaviour is potentially dangerous to themselves or others

Making judgements about when to counsel and when to refer to another agency are always difficult and it is helpful if the practitioner can talk through, in confidence, the problems of the person whom she feels may benefit from further referral. Referrals for psychiatric help are normally made through the person's general practitioner or sometimes through occupational health agencies.

What is perhaps more difficult is persuading the client that you are not the best person to help them. Suggesting referral to other agencies may be seen either as a rebuff or as a sign that you view them as being seriously mentally ill. Bearing in mind the discussion on p. 143 regarding confrontation, the person who cannot be helped through counselling *must* be approached about the possibility of referral: to do otherwise is to limit the possibilities that person has of regaining his health.

Burnout in counselling

The process of counselling and of coping with others can take its toll on the counsellor and health professional. The word **burnout** (derived from the idea that once a rocket has burnt up its fuel it is then of no use but it continues to circulate in space) has been used to denote the overall feeling that a person can experience when exhausted by being intimately involved in human relationships. Gerard Corey (cited by Murgatroyd, 1986) has suggested that there are a number of causes of burnout that the counsellor and health professional needs to bear in mind if she is to avoid it.

1. Doing the same type of helping over and over again with little variation;
2. Giving a great deal of one's own emotional and personal energy to others whilst getting very little back;
3. Being under constant pressure to produce results in a certain time scale when the time scale and the pressure are unrealistic;
4. Working with a difficult group, for example, those who are highly resistant to change, those who have been sent for help but who do not wish to be helped, or those for whom the chances of change are small because of the nature of their difficulties (for example, the terminally ill);
5. The absence of support from immediate colleagues and an abundance of criticism – what might be called 'the atmosphere of certain doubt';
6. Lack of trust between those who engage in helping and those who manage the organizational resources that make helping possible – a feature sometimes present in voluntary organizations;
7. Not having the opportunity to take new directions, to develop one's own approach or to experiment with new models of working – being unnecessarily constrained;
8. Having few opportunities for training, continuing education, supervision or support;
9. Unresolved personal conflicts beyond the helping and counselling work that interfere with the helper's ability to be effective, for example, marital problems, health problems.

Burnout in practice

Ann is a district nurse working mainly with elderly patients. Recently, her case load has increased and she has also taken on an

THE LIMITS OF COUNSELLING

Open University course. Her eldest child, who is 11 is having difficulty in settling at his new secondary school. Ann slowly finds that she is losing interest in the elderly people that she is visiting. She also finds that she is avoiding working on her Open University assignments and she begins to wonder how she had ever been interested in the course at all. Her general disenchantment is brought to a head when she visits a younger patient who begins to tell her about her marital problems. Ann realizes that she has no interest at all in what the woman has to say and just wants to leave the house. Later, Ann discontinues her Open University course and begins to consider whether or not she should remain a district nurse. She is suffering from burnout. It is only after she has had a number of long talks with her husband that she realizes the degree of emotional exhaustion that she has been experiencing. It is only then that her husband also begins to realize how difficult life has become for her. Together, they map out a plan to reorganize family life a little, so that Ann has some time for herself. Her husband agrees to take over more of the household chores and both Ann and her husband find time to sit down and listen to their son talk about his problems at school. She does not go back to the Open University course but enrolls, instead, at a local evening class. Slowly, her interest in her work returns and she feels less afraid to talk about the negative feelings she sometimes has.

It is unreasonable to suppose that we can continue to work with and for others without paying attention, also, to our own needs. The person who wants to avoid burnout needs to consider at least the following preventative measures:

1. Vary your work as much as possible;
2. Consider your education and training needs and plan ahead;
3. Take care of your physical health;
4. Consider new ways of developing counselling skills and try them out;
5. Develop an effective supervision or peer-support system;
6. Nurture your friendships and relationships with others;
7. Develop a range of interests away from work;
8. Attend refresher workshops, occasionally – as a means of updating and also as a means of experiencing new ideas and methods;
9. Initiate your own projects, without relying on others to approve them;
10. Seek positive and reliable feedback on your performance from other people.

PEER SUPPORT: CO-COUNSELLING

If we are to avoid burnout and subsequent disillusionment with the task of counselling, it is vital that we have an adequate peer-support system. Co-counselling offers one such means of ensuring that two people regularly review their life situation and their counselling practice.

Co-counselling was originally devised by Harvey Jackins in the USA (Jackins, 1965; 1970) and further developed by John Heron in the UK (Heron, 1978). Basically, it involves two people who have trained as co-counsellors meeting on a regular basis for two hours. For the first hour, one of the partners is counsellor or helper and the other is client or talker. In the second hour, roles are reversed and the counsellor becomes the client and vice versa. The counselling role in co-counselling, however, is not the traditional role of counselling: the role demands more that the person listens and gives attention to their partner than would usually be the case. In this respect, co-counselling offers a bonus to the practising counsellor in that it is an excellent way of developing and enhancing listening skills. In its most basic form, the hour spent in the role of counsellor is one of listening only, while the client verbally reviews any aspect of their life that they choose – their emotional status, life problems, recent difficulties, future plans and so forth. An important aspect of co-counselling is that what is talked about during the co-counselling sessions remains confidential to those sessions. Nothing that is talked about is discussed away from the session. For this reason, it is helpful if the two people meet only for co-counselling. To this end, co-counselling **networks** have been set up, which enable those trained to contact others.

Having the sustained and supportive attention of another person can be very liberating. It can create the circumstances in which a person is truly able to work things out for herself. Whilst the co-counselling format allows for certain verbal interventions on the part of the counsellor, those interventions never extend to giving advice, making suggestions or comparing experiences. In this sense, co-counselling is truly self-directed and client-centred. Courses in co-counselling training are usually of 40 hours in length, run either as a one-week course or as a series of evening classes. Such courses are offered by a variety of colleges and extra-mural departments of universities.

These are some of the practical problems that can occur in counselling and some methods of facing such problems and getting personal support. Sometimes it can be useful to consider some practical questions before setting out to counsel. A list of useful questions are as follows:

1. Why has this person come to me?
2. Can I help them?
3. Have I the necessary knowledge and skills to help?
4. What are my beliefs about the nature of the counselling process?
5. Why do I want to help this person?
6. Do they remind me of anyone I know? This is particularly useful when it comes to the possible development of transference and counter-transference. It is important to keep in mind the fact that this person only looks like someone else you know: they are, of course, a separate person!

PROBLEMS AND SUPPORT IN COUNSELLING AND THE HEALTH PROFESSIONAL

All of the issues discussed in this chapter apply to a wide range of situations in which health professionals may find themselves apart from the counselling situation. In other words, the issues of transference and counter-transference apply to most relationships in which professional and client develop a close relationship. The question of therapeutic distance equally applies to both counselling and all other professional relationships and so does the issue of burnout. In all aspects of health provision, the need for self- and peer-support is a particularly pertinent one. The building of a network of support throughout the professional career is a necessity if the health professional is to function effectively and caringly. In order to care effectively for others, we must learn to care for ourselves. In the next chapter, the methods of developing specific counselling skills are described in detail.

10

Learning counselling skills

ROUTES TO LEARNING

Three routes are open to the practitioner who wishes to develop a range of counselling skills: working on her own, working with a colleague or friend or learning in a small group. Each of these routes will be considered in turn and linked to the practical exercises for skills development offered in this book.

The individual working on her own

The first consideration here needs to be: what knowledge do I need in order to function as an effective counsellor? This may be answered by reference back to the three domains of knowledge referred to in Chapter 3: propositional knowledge, practical knowledge and experiential knowledge. Figure 10.1 identifies some of the types of knowledge in each of the three domains that the health professional needs to consider.

The person working on her own has a variety of options. She can, for instance, enrol on a counselling skills course. A variety of these are offered by colleges and university departments, ranging from one-year certificate courses, through two-year diploma courses to master's degree courses in counselling psychology. Such courses usually offer a wide curriculum covering both the theory and the practice of counselling.

An alternative method is for the person to train herself. This may involve attendance at a number of short counselling workshops in order to identify skilled counselling examples from effective role models, backed up by reading on the topic, reinforced by practice

Figure 10.1 Aspects of knowledge required for counselling.

Propositional knowledge
Types of counselling
Maps of the counselling process
Psychological approaches to counselling
Psychology, sociology, philosophy, politics, theology

Practical knowledge
Listening and attending skills
Counselling interventions including:
  − being prescriptive
  − being informative
  − being confronting
  − being cathartic
  − being client-centred
  − being supportive
Starting and finishing the session
Coping with transference and countertransference
Coping with silence
Avoiding burnout

Experiential knowledge
Experience of a wide range of different types of people
Experience of a wide range of human problems
Self-awareness
Life experience

---

with real clients. Such a solo programme can be helped if the individual can rely on a friend or colleague who is prepared to discuss progress and/or difficult clients. It is also helpful if the person working on her own keeps a journal in which she notes down her progress as a counsellor.

Essential to this method of training is the development of 'conscious use of self' described in Chapter 3. It is important, if progress is to be made, that the health professional works at using herself intentionally and notices what she does both in the counselling relationship and also away from it. Such noticing can bring to attention behaviours and language that are effective and those that are not. It is not until we notice what we do that we can begin to modify or change our behaviour.

Working in pairs

Perhaps a more amicable (and less lonely!) way of developing counselling skills is through working with another person. That person can be a member of the family, a friend or a colleague. It is useful if a contract is set up between the two people so that they meet at a regular time each week during which they devote that time to practising counselling skills. In the section in this book on exercises for people working in pairs (pp. 167–74), a whole range of activities is offered that can be worked through by two people. The time spent together can be divided in two and thus one person spends, say, one hour in the role of client and one hour in the role of counsellor. This style of working is not role play as the term role play suggests, i.e. acting as a person other than yourself. In the work suggested here, it is recommended that both 'client' and 'counsellor' work on real-life issues during their spell as 'client'. In this way, the self-awareness argued for in previous chapters can be enhanced, whilst counselling skills are being developed. Clearly, the subject matter discussed during these sessions must be confidential to the sessions. For this reason, it is often useful if a pair can meet solely for the purpose of practising counselling skills, though this may be difficult to arrange.

At the end of each training session, it is helpful if both parties go through a self- and peer-evaluation procedure. This involves one person verbalizing her current strengths, weaknesses and things that have been learned during the session to her partner. Then the partner offers that person both negative and positive feedback on the latter's performance during the training session. When both self and peer aspects of the evaluation process have been worked through, the two people swap roles and the process is repeated. During the self-evaluation aspects of the process, all that is required of the other person is that she listens. No comments are necessary whilst the other person is evaluating herself – that comes afterwards in the peer aspect of the process.

Regular meetings between the two partners can be further supplemented by attendance at short training workshops and by further reading on the subject of counselling, counselling psychology and psychotherapy.

Working in a group

The most effective way of training as a counsellor, outside of attendance at a formal course of training, is through the setting up of a small training group. This can be made up from colleagues who are interested in developing counselling skills and may be usefully started by the implementation of a one-day workshop to develop basic skills. Such a workshop can be run at a weekend or if a one-day slot cannot be found to suit all members of the group, the workshop can be spread over a number of meetings.

An alternative to the self-help or 'do-it-yourself' group is the more formal educational group set up by the educational body responsible for training staff in the health organization. Both groups can use the outline programme described as follows for running a counselling-skills workshop.

Figure 10.2 Stages in a counselling-skills workshop.

1. Setting the learning climate

2. Identifying the needs/wants of the group

3. Programme planning

4. Working through the programme

5. Evaluating learning

Figure 10.2 offers a sample programme outline for such a workshop on counselling skills. It may be given to workshop participants before the workshop or it may be allowed to unfold as the workshop develops. The advantage of giving it out prior to the workshop is that it offers minimal but essential structure. Many people attending workshops seem to prefer and anticipate structure and this programme can satisfy that need. On the other hand, the advantage of allowing the programme to unfold is that it ensures that the workshop is a dynamic and organic process that responds to the needs and wants of the participants as those needs and wants arise. In the end, it may be a question of the personal preference of the person setting up the workshop and, perhaps, of their previous experience in running groups of this sort.

SETTING THE LEARNING CLIMATE

This is the first stage of the counselling-skills workshop, it involves at least the following activities:

1. introductions
2. expectations
3. rationale for the workshop

The 'introductions' aspect involves helping group members to get to know one another and to remember each other's names. A variety of **icebreakers** that some people prefer to use as a means of starting the workshop are described in the literature (Brandes and Phillips, 1984; Heron, 1973; Burnard, 1985). Three examples of such icebreakers are as follows:

Example one

Group members stand up and move around the room. At a signal from the group leader, they stop and pair off with their nearest colleague. The pairs then spend a few minutes sharing their thoughts on one of the following:

1. childhood memories
2. interests away from work
3. personal interests in counselling

After a few minutes, the leader suggests that they move on and pair up with other people, with whom they then spend a few minutes discussing similar issues.

Example two

Group members, in turn, recall three positive and formative experiences from their lives and share those experiences with the rest of the group.

Example three

The group leader asks each person in turn to imagine that they were one of the following objects: a book, a piece of music or a film. The group member is then asked to describe herself as though she was

156

that object. Thus, the leader asks one of the following questions:

1. If you were a book, what book would you be? Describe yourself as that book;
2. If you were a piece of music, what piece would you be? Describe yourself as that piece of music;
3. If you were a film, what film would you be? Describe yourself as that film.

Again, the use of such icebreakers may be a question of personal preference. Some group leaders (and workshop participants) may find them difficult to use or to take part in. They seem to suit the more extraverted (and possibly younger) participants. They do, however, serve to allow people to unwind a little and thus prepare for some of the pairs and group activities described in the next section.

A quieter method of introducing a counselling-skills workshop is to invite each member in turn to identify the following things about themselves:

1. their name
2. their present job
3. their background
4. their interests away from work

After each group member has disclosed themselves to the group in this way, each member is invited to repeat his or her name slowly and in turn. This slow name-round is often usefully repeated two or three times until all members are sure of one another's names.

Following these introductory activities, group members may be invited to pair off and to discuss their expectations about the coming workshop and about future group meetings. Such expectations may include both negative and positive things. The point here is that all members be given the opportunity to explore how they feel about the coming time together and are able to share fantasies, hopes and anxieties. Following this 10-minute exercise, the group may be invited to reassemble and those expectations are discussed. It is usually helpful to discuss negative expectations first, followed by positive ones.

Once expectations have been fully explored (a process that may take from between half an hour to an hour), the group leader may offer a rationale for the workshop. That rationale will include the leader's explanation of the reasons for organizing the workshop in this manner. It will also include details of what the workshop is intended to be about. It may also include the negotiation with the group of basic ground rules for the workshop. These may include such things as:

1. rules about smoking
2. issues relating to coffee, tea and meal breaks
3. a proposal clause
4. a voluntary clause

A proposal clause raises the idea that any member of the group may feel free to propose changes to the format or structure of the group at any time. It may also be used to promote the idea of group members taking responsibility for ensuring that they get what they want from the workshop. If they are not, then they should feel free to propose a change of activity.

A voluntary clause stresses the idea that each member of the group should feel free to take part or not to take part in any aspect of the workshop or the group meetings. As all counselling workshops are organized for adults, it seems reasonable to assume that they will decide, as individuals, what does and what does not enhance their learning. It seems reasonable, too, that no part of the workshop should be compulsory.

IDENTIFYING THE NEEDS AND WANTS OF THE GROUP

The next process is one that naturally leads into programme planning. The group is invited to form into small groups of three and four. Each group brainstorms and writes down the things that they require from the workshop on a large sheet of paper. Such requirements may be particular skills, various sorts of knowledge or some sort of personal development. It is useful, too, at this stage to identify any particular resources in the group. Thus, some group members may have particular counselling exercises that they feel others may benefit from. Others may have particular knowledge about counselling theory. Figure 10.3 identifies a layout of the sheet for use in the small group.

When the small groups have had sufficient time to complete the brainstorming exercise, they may be invited to prioritize their list of needs and wants. Once this is completed, a feedback session will

Figure 10.3 Layout for a brainstorming exercise sheet.

NEEDS/WANTS	OFFERS
Identify, here, anything that you feel you need to gain from this counselling workshop	Identify, here, anything you are prepared to share with the group (skills, knowledge, activities, etc.)

ensure that group priorities are identified and offers made by individuals are recognized.

The programme for the counselling workshop develops out of the brainstorming activity. This stage involves negotiating the timing of activities required by the group. It also involves fitting in those activities with any pre-planned activites that the leader has brought to the workshop. It is useful, at this stage, to offer group members a skeleton programme plan that contains various blank spaces into which the activities identified in the brainstorming exercise can be inserted. An example of a typical programme is offered in Figure 10.4. The 'sessions' referred to in the outline programme are times when the exercises that follow in Chapter 11 may be used to develop specific counselling skills. Alternatively, those sessions can be made up of exercises offered by other group members.

WORKING THROUGH THE PROGRAMME

Once the programme has been negotiated, all that remains is for the sessions to be undertaken as planned. Given that the workshop and

Figure 10.4 Example of a skeleton counselling-skills workshop programme.

9.00 – 10.00   Introductions

10.00 – 10.30   Coffee

11.00 – 12.00   Identification of needs/wants and programme planning

12.00 – 1.00   First skills-training session

1.00 – 2.00   Lunch

2.00 – 3.00   Second skills-training session

3.00 – 3.15   Tea

3.15 – 4.15   Third skills-training session

4.15 – 5.00   Evaluation

Figure 10.5 The experiential-learning cycle applied to counselling-skills development.

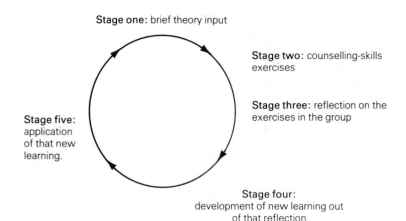

Stage one: brief theory input

Stage two: counselling-skills exercises

Stage three: reflection on the exercises in the group

Stage five: application of that new learning.

Stage four: development of new learning out of that reflection subsequent group meetings are about counselling, it is useful if the experiential-learning cycle is observed through each session (Kolb, 1984; Burnard, 1985). Experiential learning is learning through doing: through immediate, personal experience. A modification of the cycle is identified in Figure 10.5.

First, a brief theory input is offered to the group. This may be on a particular aspect of counselling or a description of a counselling skill. It is helpful, too, if the group can see some examples of excellent practice in counselling in order for them to be able to base their own counselling skills on these exemplars. Such examples of good practice may be shown on video or film or skilled practitioners may be invited to demonstrate counselling practice live, in front of the groups. This use of exemplars is particularly useful in the early stages of counselling-skills workshops and counselling-skills development. Once group members have established a basic range of their own skills, the exemplars can be dropped.

Then an activity is undertaken by the group, either as a whole or with the group divided into pairs, in order to practise a particular counselling skill. When the activity has finished (and details of how to set up and run those activities are offered with each exercise in Chapter 11), group members are invited to reflect on the experience and draw new learning from it. That learning is then applied and implications for future behaviour are discussed, it is vital that all new learning is carried over from the workshop situation to the real situation with clients: new counselling skills have to be practised as soon as possible away from the workshop to maximize the efficacy of the activity.

EVALUATING LEARNING

At the end of the workshop, the group needs to evaluate their learning. This can be done formally, through the use of a written evaluative questionnaire (Clift and Imrie, 1981; Patton, 1982) prepared prior to the workshop. Alternatively, it can be carried out through the process of self- and peer evaluation. Such self- and peer evaluation involves the following stages:

1. identification of criteria for evaluation
2. group members silently evaluating themselves using those criteria
3. group members, in turn, verbalizing their evaluation to the group

4. group members, in turn, inviting feedback from the group on their own performance during the workshop

This process may be followed by a closing round of (a) what each group member in turn liked least about the workshop, followed by a round of (b) what each member liked most about the workshop. This serves to round off the proceedings and to reinforce themes and learnings gained within the workshop.

This format for running a one-day workshop can be adapted for use in subsequent meetings of the counselling-skills learning group. At each meeting, a short period can be used to warm up the group, using icebreakers or similar activities. Then the group members can decide on what they want to achieve during the meeting. Thirdly, a series of counselling-skills exercises can be used, drawn from this book or from others (see, for example, Lewis and Streitfield, 1971; Pfeiffer and Jones, 1974 and ongoing; Wilkinson and Canter, 1982; Heron, 1973; Egan, 1986a). After each exercise, a reflective period can be instituted to allow consideration of how the new skill may be implemented in the real situation. Finally, the meeting can close with an evaluation activity.

These, then, are three approaches to counselling-skills training that can be used separately or in combination. All three emphasize the need for practice and for practical experience. All three need to be combined with constant reflection on the qualities of the effective counsellor. Counselling without certain skills can be fruitless. Skills without human qualities will be mechanical. All health professionals who practise counselling as an aspect of their job need to consider a balance between counselling skills, up-to-date knowledge and the development of a human and caring approach to people.

LEARNING COUNSELLING SKILLS AND THE
HEALTH PROFESSIONAL

As we have noted throughout this book, the skills described as counselling skills also have wider application outside the counselling relationship and can be used to enhance professional practice in any branches of the caring and health professions. The format for organizing the learning of counselling skills described in this chapter can also be adapted and used for learning or developing a whole range of interpersonal skills related to health care including interviewing, stress management, self-awareness, assertiveness, assessment and evaluation.

11

Counselling-skills exercises

In Chapter 10, details were given as to how to develop counselling skills when working alone, in pairs or in a small group. This chapter offers a range of counselling-skills exercises and activities. The first set consists of those for the individual working on her own, the second set for people working in pairs and the third for people working in groups. The second and third sets may be used in combination by a group of colleagues working together to enhance their counselling skills. Each exercise should be worked through slowly with plenty of time allowed for processing or discussing the activity afterwards.

As we noted in the previous chapter, a useful format for a counselling-skills training session is as follows:

1. identification of how the group wants to spend the time
2. a theory input and some examples of good counselling practice, either live or shown on video or film
3. using a variety of exercises to develop counselling skills
4. evaluation activities

The exercises that follow will serve as the exercises to develop counselling skills. Built into each of the pairs exercises and group exercises are the means to evaluate learning at the end of each activity. It is recommended that the evaluation procedure is followed fairly closely so that the maximum amount of learning may be gained from each exercise. No claims are made that this list of exercises is exhaustive of all possible exercises and many more may be gleaned from the literature listed in the bibliography. Many exercises may also be developed by group members, themselves.

The 'pairs' format is particularly useful. In this, the group divides up into pairs, each member of which spends some time in the role of counsellor and that of client. After a period of practising specific counselling skills, the partners swap roles. This format can be used on a regular basis for practising counselling and may be combined with receiving feedback on skills development from the partner.

All of the work done individually, in pairs or in a group must be followed up quickly by real life experience. Thus the counsellor must learn to develop the conscious use of self referred to throughout this book. In this way, the health professional can make full use of any learning gained by putting it into practice in real counselling situations. Like all skills, counselling skills must be reinforced if they are to become a regular part of the person's repertoire of behaviour.

EXERCISES FOR THE PERSON WORKING ON HER OWN

Exercise 1

Aim of the exercise To clarify beliefs and values, prior to undertaking counselling.

Process of the exercise Write out in a free style a paper that expresses your current set of values and beliefs about human beings, counselling and about yourself. Do not try to make the paper academic in any way and do not worry about style or presentation. Once you have written the paper, consider whether or not it highlights any ambiguities or contradictions in our construing of the world. If so, consider whether or not you will attempt to resolve those contradictions. Consider, also, ways in which your beliefs and values affect your work and your attitude towards counselling. You may or may not choose to show the paper to someone else and have them comment on it.

Exercise 2

Aim of the exercise To consider aspects of yourself and your work that will help or hinder your counselling.

Process of the exercise Brainstorm onto a sheet of paper all those aspects of yourself and your work that you bring to your counselling. Include in your list those aspects of yourself and your work that you anticipate will cause difficulties. Allow yourself to think and write quickly. Once the list has become fairly lengthy, organize it into 'pluses' and 'minuses'. Consider, then, the degree to which one list is longer than the other and the implications of that. Consider, also, what you intend to do about the minuses.

Exercise 3

Aim of the exercise To enable a continuous means of personal evaluation to be maintained.

Process of the exercise Keep a journal from the point of taking up counselling. Use the following headings to order the journal:

1. recent skills developed
2. recent problems encountered and problem-solving methods used
3. new references to books and journals noted
4. aspects of personal growth.

Journals may usefully be kept by all members of a group working together on developing counselling skills. At each meeting of the group, time can be set aside to discuss journal entries.

Exercise 4

Aim of the exercise To develop conscious use of self.

Process of the exercise Set aside a time each day when you notice what it is you do and how you do it. Notice patterns of behaviour, speech, proximity to others, use of touch, hand and arm gestures, social skills and so on. Try out new behaviour and new counselling skills as they develop. Allow this time to develop and lengthen until you become more aware of how you react and interact.

Exercise 5

Aim of the exercise To develop the ability of noticing.

Process of the exercise Noticing (sometimes called 'staying awake' or 'conscious awareness') involves setting aside time each day to notice everything that is going on around you. Notice sounds, smells, colours, activity, objects and so on. Allow this period of noticing to develop and lengthen. Use the activity, particularly, when you are with other people.

Exercise 6

Aim of the exercise To develop observational skills, conscious use of self and the ability to notice.

Process of the exercise Spend 20 minutes each evening, sitting in the same place at the same time. Allow your attention to focus only on those things that you see, hear, smell or feel, outside of yourself. Do not attempt to evaluate what comes in through your senses, but only notice them. Regular use of this activity (akin to certain types of meditation) will improve your ability to keep your attention out and will improve your observational skills.

Exercise 7

Aim of the exercise To experience physical changes in the body, to become more aware of the body and to physically relax.

Process of the exercise Find a place that is quiet and warm in which you can lie down for about half an hour, undisturbed. Once you are lying down, take three deep breaths. Then allow your attention to focus on the muscles in your face. Let them relax. Then focus your attention on the muscles in your shoulders and upper arms. Let them relax. Focus your attention on the muscles in your lower arms and hands. Stretch out your fingers. Then let your arms relax. Then focus your attention on the muscles in your chest and stomach. Let those muscles relax. Then focus on the muscles in your legs and stretch your feet forward. Then let all the muscles in your legs relax. Then notice how all the muscles in your body are relaxed. Allow yourself to notice what it feels like to be relaxed. Notice, too, parts of the body that you find difficult to relax. After about 10 minutes, stretch gently, allow yourself to sit up and then slowly, stand up. Notice the difference in the way you feel before and after the activity.

This exercise may also be used as a stress-reduction activity with clients who find it difficult to relax. It can also be dictated onto a tape for use as a means of deep relaxation.

Exercise 8

Aim of the exercise To identify personal strengths and weaknesses in terms of counselling interventions.

Process of the exercise Consider Heron's (1986) six category intervention analysis:

1. prescriptive interventions: giving advice, offering suggestions
2. informative interventions: offering information
3. confronting interventions: challenging
4. cathartic interventions: helping the client to express emotion
5. catalytic interventions: 'drawing out' the client
6. supportive interventions: encouraging, validating the client

Identify the two categories that you feel you are least skilled in using at the moment. Then consider the two categories that you are most skilled in using at the moment. Consider the implications of your assessment and anticipate ways that you can enhance your deficiencies.

Exercise 9

Aim of the exercise To plan future objectives.

Process of the exercise Write down a list of the counselling skills or aspects of counselling that you need to improve upon. Make each of them a specific, behavioural objective and one that is attainable. Then determine how you will meet those objectives.

EXERCISES FOR PEOPLE WORKING IN PAIRS

A and B denote the individuals within each pair.

Exercise 10

Aim of the exercise To experience problems associated with listening.

Equipment required/environmental considerations The pair should sit facing each other in chairs of equal height. It is helpful if the room is comfortably warm and free from distractions and interruptions.

Process of the exercise A talks to B on any subject for 4 minutes and B does not listen! The roles are then reversed and B talks to A, who also does not listen! After the second round the pair discuss the activity.

Evaluation procedure At the end of the exercise each person should report to the other what they disliked and what they liked about the activity. They may also comment on what they will be able to carry over from it into the real counselling situation.

Exercise 11

Aim of the exercise To experience problems with the nonverbal aspects of listening.

Equipment required/environmental considerations The pair should sit facing each other in chairs of equal height. It is helpful if the room is comfortably warm and free from distractions and interruptions.

Process of the exercise A talks to B for 4 minutes about any topic and B listens but contradicts the first four aspects of the SOLER behaviours (see p. 111) identified by Egan (1986b). Thus, B does not sit squarely in relation to A. She folds her arms and her legs. She leans away from her partner and makes no eye contact with her. After 4 minutes, roles are reversed and B talks to A, while A listens but offers contradictory behaviours. After the second round, the pair discuss the exercise.

Evaluation procedure At the end of the exercise each person should report to the other what they disliked and what they liked about the activity. They may also comment on what they will be able to carry over from it into the real counselling situation.

Exercise 12

Aim of the exercise To experience effective listening and to enhance listening skills.

Equipment required/environmental considerations The pair should sit facing each other in chairs of equal height. It is helpful if the room is comfortably warm and free from distractions and interruptions.

Process of the exercise A talks to B for 4 minutes about any topic and B listens, observing the SOLER behaviours. Thus, she sits squarely in an open position. She leans slightly towards her partner and maintains good eye contact. She also relaxes and does nothing but listen. It is important that this is not a conversation but a listening exercise! After 4 minutes, roles are reversed and B talks to A, who listens appropriately. The pair then discuss the exercise and compare it with the previous two exercises.

Evaluation procedure At the end of the exercise each person should report to the other what they disliked and what they liked about the activity. They may also comment on what they will be able to carry out from it into the real counselling situation.

Exercise 13

Aim of the exercise To practise effective listening and to evaluate the effectiveness of the listening.

Equipment required/environmental considerations The pair should sit facing each other in chairs of equal height. It is helpful if the room is comfortably warm and free from distractions and interruptions.

Process of the exercise A talks to B for 4 minutes on any topic. B listens and periodically recaps what A has said, to A's satisfaction. After 4 minutes, roles are reversed and B talks to A, who listens and periodically recaps. Afterwards, the pair discuss the exercise.

Evaluation procedure At the end of the exercise each person should report to the other what they disliked and what they liked about the activity. They may also comment on what they will be able to carry over from it into the real counselling situation.

Exercise 14

Aim of the exercise To discriminate between open and closed questions.

Equipment required/environmental considerations The pair should sit facing each other in chairs of equal height. It is helpful if the room is comfortably warm and free from distractions and interruptions. A pencil and paper are needed for this activity.

Process of the exercise Both partners jot down the following sequence: OOCCOCOC. A then asks B questions on any of the following topics:

1. current issues at work
2. recent holidays
3. the current political situation

The questions are asked in the sequence noted previously (i.e. open question, open question, closed question, closed question and so on), until all the questions have been asked. Then the pair swap roles and B asks questions of A, in that sequence and on one of those topics.

Evaluation procedure At the end of the exercise each person should report to the other what they disliked and what they liked about the activity. They may also comment on what they will be able to carry over from it into the real counselling situation.

Exercise 15

Aim of the exercise To practise 'funnelling' in questioning.

Equipment required/environmental considerations The pair should sit facing each other in chairs of equal height. It is helpful if the room is comfortably warm and free from distractions and interruptions.

Process of the exercise A asks questions of B on any subject they wish starting with a very broad open question and slowly allowing the questions to become more specific and focused. After 4 minutes, the pairs swap roles and B asks questions of A, moving from the general to the particular.

Evaluation procedure At the end of the exercise each person should report to the other what they disliked and what they liked about the activity. They may also comment on what they will be able to carry over from it into the real counselling situation.

Exercise 16

Aim of the exercise To practise reflection and selective reflection.

Equipment required/environmental considerations The pair should sit facing each other in chairs of equal height. It is helpful if the room is comfortably warm and free from distractions and interruptions.

Process of the exercise A talks to B about any subject and A uses only reflection or selective reflection to encourage her to continue. This should be carried on for about 6 minutes. After 6 minutes, roles are reversed and B talks to A, who uses only reflection or selective reflection as a response. For details of these two techniques, see Chapter 7 on client-centred counselling skills.

Evaluation procedure At the end of the exercise, each person should report to the other what they disliked and what they liked about the activity. They may also comment on what they will be able to carry over from it into the real counselling situation.

Exercise 17

Aim of the exercise To practise a range of client-centred counselling skills.

Equipment required/environmental considerations The pair should sit facing each other in chairs of equal height. It is helpful if the room is comfortably warm and free from distractions and interruptions.

Process of the exercise A begins to counsel B but restricts herself to the following types of interventions only:

1. open or closed questions
2. reflections or selective reflections
3. checking for understanding
4. empathy-building statements

The counselling session should continue for at least 10 minutes, then both partners change roles for a further 10 minutes. There should be no sense of play-acting or role-playing about the exercise. Both partners should counsel on real issues and thus develop realistic skills. This exercise, like the previous one, is very difficult because both parties are 'in the know'!

Evaluation procedure At the end of the exercise, each person should report to the other what they disliked and what they liked about the activity. They may also comment on what they will be able to carry over from it into the real counselling situation.

Exercise 18

Aim of the exercise To experience being asked a wide range of questions.

Equipment required/environmental considerations The pair should sit facing each other in chairs of equal height. It is helpful if the room is comfortably warm and free from distractions and interruptions.

Process of the exercise A asks a wide range of questions, on any topic at all for 5 minutes and B does not respond to them or answer them! After 5 minutes, roles are reversed and B asks questions of A, who does not respond to them. It is important for both partners to notice how they feel about asking and being asked very personal questions.

Evaluation procedure At the end of the exercise each person should report to the other what they disliked and what they liked about the activity. They may also comment on what they will be able to carry over from it into the real counselling situation.

Exercise 19

Aim of the exercise To notice the difference between being asked questions and making statements.

Equipment required/environmental considerations The pair should sit facing each other in chairs of equal height. It is helpful if the room is comfortably warm and free from distractions and interruptions.

Process of the exercise A sits and makes a series of statements on any topic to B for 5 minutes. B listens to the statements but does not respond to them. After 5 minutes, roles are reversed and B makes a series of statements to A who listens only. Afterwards, the pair discuss the perceived differences between how this exercise felt and how the previous one felt. They discuss, also, the relative merits of questions and statements with regard to counselling.

Evaluation procedure At the end of the exercise each person should report to the other what they disliked and what they liked about the activity. They may also comment on what they will be able to carry over from it into the real counselling situation.

Exercise 20

Aim of the exercise To explore personal history.

Equipment required/environmental considerations The pair should sit facing each other in chairs of equal height. It is helpful if the room is comfortably warm and free from distractions and interruptions.

Process of the exercise A talks to B for 10 minutes and reviews her life history to date. Any aspects may be included or left out but some sort of chronological order should be aimed at. After 10 minutes, roles are reversed and B reviews her biography to date, while A listens but does not comment.

Evaluation procedure At the end of the exercise each person should report to the other what they disliked and what they liked about the activity. They may also comment on what they will be able to carry over from it into the real counselling situation.

Exercise 21

Aim of the exercise To explore 'free association'.

Equipment required/environmental considerations The pair should sit facing each other in chairs of equal height. It is helpful if the room is comfortably warm and free from distractions and interruptions.

Process of the exercise A sits and verbalizes whatever comes into her head, whilst B sits and listens only. Everything possible should be verbalized, but A should note the things that she does not verbalize! This process continues for 3 minutes when the pair swap roles and B attempts free association accompanied by A's attention and listening. Afterwards, the pair discuss the implications of the activity for themselves and for their counselling practice.

Evaluation procedure At the end of the exercise each person should report to the other what they disliked and what they liked about the activity. They may also comment on what they will be able to carry over from it into the real counselling situation.

Exercise 22

Aim of the exercise To self-evaluate.

Equipment required/environmental considerations The pair should sit facing each other in chairs of equal height. It is helpful if the room is comfortably warm and free from distractions and interruptions.

Process of the exercise A considers and verbalizes all the positive and negative aspects of her counselling practice to date. Negative considerations should be made first. When A has finished B goes through the same process. Afterwards, the pair consider the implications of their evaluations for their counselling practice.

Evaluation procedure At the end of the exercise each person should report to the other what they disliked and what they liked about the activity. They may also comment on what they will be able to carry over from it into the real counselling situation.

Exercise 23

Aim of the exercise To receive feedback on counselling skills.

Equipment required/environmental considerations The pair should sit facing each other in chairs of equal height. It is helpful if the room is comfortably warm and free from distractions and interruptions.

Process of the exercise A offers B both positive and negative feedback as to how she perceives the other's counselling skills. Negative comments should be made first. Then B offers A feedback on her counselling skills. Afterwards, both partners consider the implications of this feedback for their counselling practice and compare it with their own, self-evaluation.

Evaluation procedure At the end of the exercise each person should report to the other what they disliked and what they liked about the activity. They may also comment on what they will be able to carry over from it into the real counselling situation.

EXERCISES FOR PEOPLE WORKING IN GROUPS

Exercise 24

Aim of the exercise To increase the listening and attending skills of group members.

Number of participants Any number between 5 and 20.

Time required Between 1 and 1½ hours.

Equipment required/environmental considerations The group should sit in chairs of equal height and in a circle. It is helpful if the room is comfortably warm and does not contain too many distractions.

Process of the exercise The group holds a discussion on any topic. One ground rule applies throughout the exercise: once the first person has spoken, before anyone else contributes to the discussion, they must first summarize what the person before them has said, to that person's satisfaction! After half an hour, the group discusses the activity.

Evaluation procedure Learning from the exercise is evaluated by two rounds. First, each person in turn says what she did not like about the exercise. Then, each person in turn says what she did like about the activity. A third round can be used to establish how each person will use the learning gained, in the future.

Variations on the exercise

1. The facilitator chooses a topic for discussion, for example:
   (a) qualities of the effective counsellor
   (b) how we can become better counsellors
   (c) how this group is developing
2. The group can divide into smaller groups of 4 or 5 people to carry out the exercise and then have a plenary session back in the larger group.

Exercise 25

Aim of the exercise To practise asking questions in a group and to experience being asked questions.

Number of participants Any number between 5 and 20.

Time required Between 1 and 1½ hours.

Equipment required/environmental considerations The group should sit in chairs of equal height and in a circle. It is helpful if the room is comfortably warm and does not contain too many distractions.

Process of the exercise Each person, in turn, spends 5 minutes in the 'hotseat'. When occupying the hotseat, they may be asked questions, on any subject, by any member of the group. If they do not wish to answer a particular question, they may say 'pass'. At the end of the person's 5 minutes in the hotseat, she nominates the next person to occupy it, until all members of the group have had a turn.

Evaluation procedure Learning from the exercise is evaluated by two rounds. First, each person in turn says what she did not like about the exercise. Then, each person in turn says what she did like about the activity. A third round can be used to establish how each person will use the learning gained, in the future.

Variations on the exercise

1. The time in the hotseat may be varied from 2 to 10 minutes depending upon the size of the group and the time available.
2. A large group may be split into smaller groups.
3. With a group in which members know each other very well, the 'pass' facility should be abandoned!

Exercise 26

Aim of the exercise To experience clear communication within the group.

Number of participants Any number between 5 and 20.

Time required Between 1 and 1½ hours.

Equipment required/environmental considerations The group should sit in chairs of equal height and in a circle. It is helpful if the room is comfortably warm and does not contain too many distractions.

Process of the exercise The group holds a discussion on any topic and observes the following ground rules:

1. Speak directly, using 'I' rather than 'you', 'we' or 'one'.
2. Speak directly to others, using the first person.
3. Stay in the present.

4. Avoid theorizing about what is going on in the group.

Either the facilitator acts as guardian of the ground rules, or the group monitors itself.

Evaluation procedure Learning from the exercise is evaluated by two rounds. First, each person in turn says what she did not like about the exercise. Then, each person in turn says what she did like about the activity. A third round can be used to establish how each person will use the learning gained, in the future.

Variations on the exercise No topic is chosen by or for the group: the material for discussion evolves out of what is happening in the here-and-now.

Exercise 27

Aim of the exercise To experience participation in a 'leaderless' group and to consider the dynamics of such an activity.

Number of participants Any number between 5 and 20.

Time required Between 1 and 1½ hours.

Equipment required/environmental considerations The group should sit in chairs of equal height and in a circle. It is helpful if the room is comfortably warm and does not contain too many distractions. An object to use as a 'conch' is required.

Process of the exercise The group have a discussion on any topic. In order to speak, however, they must be in possession of the conch – an object that signifies that at that moment, the person holding it is leading the group. Other people who wish to speak must nonverbally negotiate for possession of the conch. After about half an hour, the group drop the 'conch' rule and freely discuss the activity.

Evaluation procedure Learning from the exercise is evaluated by two rounds. First, each person in turn says what she did not like about the exercise. Then, each person in turn says what she did like about the activity. A third round can be used to establish how each person will use the learning gained, in the future.

Variations on the exercise

1. The facilitator chooses a topic for the group to discuss.
2. A rule may be introduced whereby each person may only make one statement when in possession of the conch.

Exercise 28

Aim of the exercise To practise using client-centred counselling interventions in a group.

Number of participants Any number between 5 and 20.

Time required Between 1 and 1½ hours.

Equipment required/environmental considerations The group should sit in chairs of equal height and in a circle. It is helpful if the room is comfortably warm and does not contain too many distractions.

Process of the exercise The group members are only allowed to: (a) ask questions of each other, (b) practise reflections, (c) offer empathy-building statements or (d) check for understanding of each other. After half an hour, the group discusses the exercise, having dropped the rule about types of interventions.

Evaluation procedure Learning from the exercise is evaluated by two rounds. First, each person in turn says what she did not like about the exercise. Then each person in turn says what she did like about the activity. A third round can be used to establish how each person will use the learning gained, in the future.

Variations on the exercise

1. One group member is invited to facilitate a general discussion with the group, using only: (a) questions, (b) reflections, (c) empathy-building statements or (d) checking for understanding. Afterwards, the group offers that person feedback on her performance.
2. Group members, in turn, facilitate a discussion using only the aforementioned types of interventions for periods of 10 minutes each.

Exercise 29

Aim of the exercise To explore silence in a group context.

Number of participants Any number between 5 and 20.

Time required Between 1 and 1½ hours.

Equipment required/environmental considerations The group should sit in chairs of equal height and in a circle. It is helpful if the room is comfortably warm and does not contain too many distractions.

Process of the exercise The group facilitator suggests to the group that they sit in total silence for a period of 5 minutes. When the 5 minutes is over, the group discuss the experience.

Evaluation procedure Learning from the exercise is evaluated by two rounds. First, each person in turn says what she did not like about the exercise. Then, each person in turn says what she did like about the activity. A third round can be used to establish how each person will use the learning gained, in the future.

Variations on the exercise The group may sit in silence with their eyes closed.

Exercise 30

Aim of the exercise To explore a variety of facets of counselling.

Number of participants Any number between 5 and 20.

Time required Between 1 and 1½ hours.

Equipment required/environmental considerations The group should sit in chairs of equal height and in a circle. It is helpful if the room is comfortably warm and does not contain too many distractions. A large sheet of paper or a black or white board is required for this activity.

Process of the exercise The group carries out a brainstorming activity. One member of the group acts as 'scribe' and jots down on a large sheet of paper or a black or white board all comments from the group on one of the following topics. No contributions are

179

discarded and group members are to be encouraged to call out any associations that they make with the topic:

1. qualities of an effective counsellor
2. problems/difficulties of this group
3. activities for improving counselling skills
4. qualities of an ineffective counsellor
5. skills required for effective counselling
6. problems that health professionals are likely to encounter in counselling

Evaluation procedure Learning from the exercise is evaluated by two 'rounds'. First, each person in turn says what she did not like about the exercise. Then, each person in turn says what she did like about the activity. A third round can be used to establish how each person will use the learning gained, in the future.

Exercise 31

Aim of the exercise To receive feedback from other group members.

Number of participants Any number between 5 and 20.

Time required Between 1 and 1½ hours.

Equipment required/environmental considerations The group should sit in chairs of equal height and in a circle. It is helpful if the room is comfortably warm and does not contain too many distractions.

Process of the exercise Each member of the group, listens to other members of the group offering her positive feedback, i.e. things they like about that person. The feedback is given in the form of a round, with each person in turn offering feedback until every group member has spoken. The group member receiving feedback is not allowed to respond to the comments but must listen in silence!

Evaluation procedure Learning from the exercise is evaluated by two rounds. First, each person in turn says what she did not like about the exercise. Then, each person in turn says what she did like about the activity. A third round can be used to establish how each person will use the learning gained, in the future.

Variations on the exercise With a group in which members know each other very well, a round of negative feedback may be offered to each group member, if they require it. This activity should be handled with care!

Exercise 32

Aim of the exercise To carry out a self- and peer evaluation.

Number of participants Any number between 5 and 20.

Time required Between 1 and 1½ hours.

Equipment required/environmental considerations The group should sit in chairs of equal height and in a circle. It is helpful if the room is comfortably warm and does not contain too many distractions.

Process of the exercise The group identify six criteria for evaluating members of the group, for example:

1. contribution to activities
2. self-disclosure
3. contribution of new ideas to the group etc.

Then each group member silently jots down her own evaluation of herself under these six headings. When all members have finished, each reads out their notes to the rest of the group and invites feedback from other group members on those six criteria. The process is repeated until all group members have both verbalized their evaluation and received feedback from other group members.

Evaluation procedure Learning from the exercise is evaluated by two rounds. First, each person in turn says what she did not like about the exercise. Then, each person in turn says what she did like about the activity. A third round can be used to establish how each person will use the learning gained, in the future.

Variations on the exercise The feedback from the group may be offered systematically: each group member in turn working round the group offers the individual feedback on her performance.

Exercise 33

Aim of the exercise To explore a spontaneous and leaderless group activity: the 'Quaker' group.

Number of participants Any number between 5 and 20.

Time required Between 1 and 1½ hours.

Equipment required/environmental considerations The group should sit in chairs of equal height and in a circle. It is helpful if the room is comfortably warm and does not contain too many distractions.

Process of the exercise The group has no topic for discussion and no leader. Group members are encouraged to verbalize what they are feeling and what they are thinking as those thoughts and feelings occur but there is no obligation for anyone else to respond to the statements offered. The group may fall into silence at times and at other times be very noisy! The group exercise should be allowed to run for at least three-quarters of an hour. After that period, group members can freely discuss how it felt to take part in the activity.

Evaluation procedure Learning from the exercise is evaluated by two rounds. First, each person in turn says what she did not like about the exercise. Then, each person in turn says what she did like about the activity. A third round can be used to establish how each person will use the learning gained, in the future.

Variations on the exercise A topic may be chosen for the group to consider, but no direction is offered by the group facilitator and group members make statements about the topic as and when they choose.

COUNSELLING SKILLS AND THE HEALTH PROFESSIONAL

These are a range of counselling-skills exercises that have been used by the author in a variety of contexts to help in the development of counselling and interpersonal skills. They can be modified and adapted to suit the specific needs of particular groups of health professionals. Nurses, doctors, physiotherapists, occupational therapists, speech therapists, voluntary workers, social workers and others can all use the activities described here. Often, too, as we have noted, the best exercises are those that you devise yourself: the group that learns to identify its particular needs and then develops exercises to explore a particular skill can quickly become an autonomous learning group. During workshops, it is useful if the following questions can be considered by those present as a means of focusing and evaluating the learning taking place:

1. What do I need to do to enhance my counselling skills?
2. What client groups are likely to need the different sorts of counselling approaches?
3. How can I enhance my own self-awareness?
4. How self-aware am I?
5. What are my strengths and weaknesses as a counsellor?
6. What personal qualities do I offer as a counsellor?

These sorts of questions can either be discussed in pairs by workshop participants or can be the topic of a larger group discussion. They are questions that can be returned to during the workshop or during a series of study days.

Learning to practise as a counsellor can be an exciting and challenging process. It is hoped that this book has offered some signposts towards directions in which counselling expertise may be gained by the health professional. The rest is up to the individual or the group. Good luck!

References

Alberti, R.E. and Emmons, M.L. (1982) *Your Perfect Right: A Guide to Assertive Living*, 4th edn. Impact Publishers, San Luis, California.

Alexander, F.M. (1969) *Resurrection of the Body*. University Books, New York.

Argyle, M. (1975) *The Psychology of Interpersonal Behaviour*. Penguin, Harmondsworth.

Bandler, R. and Grinder, J. (1975) *The Structure of Magic. Vol. 1. A Book About Language and Therapy*. Science and Behaviour Books, California.

Bandler, R. and Grinder, J. (1982) *Reframing: Neuro-Linguistic Programming and the Transformation of Meaning*. Real People Press, Moab, Utah.

Bannister, D. and Fransella, F. (1986) *Inquiring Man*, 3rd edn. Croom Helm, London.

Beck, A., Rush, A., Shaw, B. and Emery, C. (1979) *Cognitive Therapy of Depression*. Wiley, Chichester.

Berne, E. (1964) *Games People Play*. Penguin, Harmondsworth.

Berne, E. (1972) *What Do You Say After You Say Hello?* Corgi, London.

Bowlby, J. (1975) *Separation*. Penguin, Harmondsworth.

Brandes, D. and Phillips, R. (1984) *The Gamester's Handbook. Vol. 2.* Hutchinson, London.

Brown, R. (1986) *Social Psychology*, 3rd edn. Collier Macmillan, New York.

Buber, M. (1948) *Tales of Hassidism: the Later Masters*. Schoken, New York.

Buber, M. (1958) *I and Thou*. Scribner, New York.

Buber, M. (1966) *The Knowledge of Man: a Philosophy of the Interhuman*, M. Freidman (ed.), R.G. Smith (trans.). Harper and Row, New York.

Bugental, E.K. and Bugental, J.F.T. (1984) Dispiritedness: a new perspective on a familiar state. *Journal of Humanistic Psychology*, **24**, 46–67.

Bugental, J.F.T. (1980) The far side of despair. *Journal of Humanistic Psychology*, **20**, 49–68.

Burnard, P. (1985) *Learning Human Skills: a Guide for Nurses*. Heinemann, London.

Burnard, P. and Morrison, P. (1987) Nurses' perceptions of their interpersonal skills. *Nursing Times*, **23**, 59.

Campbell, A.V. (1984) *Paid to Care?* SPCK, London.

Carkuff, R.R. (1969) *Helping and Human Relations. Vol. 1. Selection and Training*. Holt, Rinehart and Winston, New York.

Chapman, A.J. and Gale, A. (1982) *Psychology and People: a Tutorial Text*. British Psychological Society/Macmillan Press, London.

Claxton, G. (1984) *Live and Learn: an Introduction to the Psychology of Growth and Change in Everyday Life*. Harper and Row, London.

Clift, J.C. and Imrie, B.W. (1981) *Assessing Students: Appraising Teaching*. Croom Helm, London.

Cox, M. (1978) *Structuring the Therapeutic Process*. Pergamon Press, London.

Dewey, J. (1916) (1966) *Democracy and Education*, Free Press, London.

Dewey, J. (1938) (1971) *Experience and Education*. Collier Macmillan, London.

Egan, G. (1982) *The Skilled Helper*, 2nd edn. Brooks/Cole, Monterey, California.

Egan, G. (1986a) *Exercises in Helping Skills*, 3rd edn. Brooks/Cole, Monterey, California.

Egan, G. (1986b) *The Skilled Helper*, 3rd edn. Brooks/Cole, Monterey, California.

Ellis, A. (1962) *Reason and Emotion in Psychotherapy*. Lyle, Stuart, New York.

ENB (1982) *Syllabus of Training: Professional Register – Part 3: (Registered Mental Nurse)*. English and Wales National Boards for Nursing, Midwifery and Health Visiting, London and Cardiff.

Epting, T.R. (1984) *Personal Construct Counselling and Psychotherapy*. Wiley, Chichester.

Erikson, E. (1959) *Identity and the Life Cycle*. International Universities Press, New York.

Ernst, S. and Goodison, L. (1981) *In Our Own Hands: a Book of Self-help Therapy*. The Women's Press, London.

Fay, A. (1976) Clinical notes on paradoxical therapy. *Psychotherapy: Theory, Research and Practice*, **18**, 14–22.

Fay, A. (1978) *Making Things Better by Making Them Worse*. Hawthorne, New York.

Fiedler, F.E. (1950) The concept of an ideal therapeutic relationship, *Journal of Consulting Psychology*, **14**, 239–45.

Feldenkrais, M. (1972) *Awareness Through Movement*. Harper and Row, New York.

Fordham, F. (1966) *An Introduction to Jung's Psychology*. Penguin, Harmondsworth.

Frankl, V.E. (1959) *Man's Search for Meaning*. Beacon Press, New York.

Frankl, V.E. (1960) Paradoxical intention: a logotherapeutic technique, *American Journal of Psychotherapy*, **14**, 520–35.

Frankl, V.E. (1969) *The Will to Meaning*. World Publishing Co., New York.

Frankl, V.E. (1975) *The Unconscious God*. Simon and Schuster, New York.

Frankl, V.E. (1978) *The Unheard Cry for Meaning*. Simon and Schuster, New York.

Hall, C. (1954) *A Primer of Freudian Psychology*. Mentor Books, New York.

Halmos, P. (1965) *The Faith of the Counsellors*. Constable, London.

Harris, T. (1973) *I'm OK. You're OK*. Pan, London.

Haydn, H. (1965) Humanism in 1984. *The American Scholar*, **35**, 12–27.

Haywood, J. (1975) *Information: a Prescription Against Pain*. RCN, London.

Heron, J. (1970) *The phenomenology of the gaze*. Human Potential Research Project, University of Surrey, Guildford, Surrey.

Heron, J. (1973) *Experiential Training Techniques*. Human Potential Research Project, University of Surrey, Guildford, Surrey.

Heron, J. (1977a) *Catharsis in Human Development*. Human Potential

Research Project, University of Surrey, Guildford, Surrey.

Heron, J. (1977b) *Behaviour Analysis in Education and Training.* Human Potential Research Project, University of Surrey, Guildford, Surrey.

Heron, J. (1978) *Co-Counselling Teacher's Manual.* Human Potential Research Project, University of Surrey, Guildford, Surrey.

Heron, J. (1981) Philosophical basis for a new paradigm, in P. Reason and J. Rowans (eds), *Human Inquiry: a Sourcebook of New Paradigm Research.* Wiley, Chichester.

Heron, J. (1986) Six category intervention analysis, 2nd edn. *Human Potential Research Project,* University of Surrey, Guildford, Surrey.

Hesse, H. (1927) *Steppenwolf.* Penguin, Harmondsworth.

Hesse, H. (1979) *My Belief.* Panther, St Albans.

Hopkins, G.M. (1953) *Poems and Prose* (W.H. Gardner ed.). Penguin, Harmondsworth.

Jackins, H. (1965) *The Human Side of Human Beings.* Rational Island Publishers, Seattle, Washington.

Jackins, H. (1970) *Fundamentals of Co-counselling Manual.* Rational Island Publishers, Seattle, Washington.

James, M. and Jongeward, D. (1971) *Born to Win: Transactional Analysis with Gestalt Experiments.* Addison-Wesley, Reading, Mass.

Jourard, S.M. (1964) *The Transparent Self.* Van Nostrand, Princeton, New Jersey.

Jourard, S.M. (1971) *Self-Disclosure: An Experimental Study of the Transparent Self.* Wiley, New York.

Jung, C.G. (1978) *Selected Writings* (A. Storr ed.). Fontana, London.

Kahn, R.L. and Cannell, C.F. (1957) *The Dynamics of Interviewing.* Wiley, New York.

Kalisch, B.J. (1971) Strategies for developing nurse empathy. *Nursing Outlook,* **19**, 714–17.

Kelly, G. (1955) *The Psychology of Personal Constructs. Vols 1 and 2.* Norton, New York.

Kelly, G. (1969) The autobiography of a theory. In B. Maher (ed.) *Clinical Psychology and Personality: the Selected Papers of George Kelly.* Wiley, New York.

Kolb, D. (1984) *Experiential Learning.* Prentice Hall, Englewood Cliffs, New Jersey.

Kopp, S. (1974) *If You Meet the Buddha on the Road, Kill Him!: a Modern Pilgrimage through Myth, Legend and Psychotherapy.* Sheldon Press, London.

Laing, R.D. (1959) *The Divided Self.* Penguin, Harmondsworth.

Lewis, H. and Streitfield, H. (1971) *Growth Games.* Bantam Books, New York.

Lowen, A. (1967) *Betrayal of the Body.* Macmillan, New York.

Lowen, A. and Lowen, L. (1977) *The Way to Vibrant Health: a Manual of Bioenergetic Exercises.* Harper and Row, New York.

Luft, J. (1969) *Of Human Interaction: the Johari Model.* Mayfield, Palo Alto, California.

Mcquarrie, J. (1973) *Existentialism.* Pelican, Harmondsworth.

Marriage Guidance Council (1983) *Aims, Beliefs and Organisation.* The National Marriage Guidance Council, Rugby, Warwickshire.

May, R. (1983a) The problem of evil: an open letter to Carl Rogers. *Journal of Humanistic Psychology*, **122**, 10–21.

May, R. (1983b) *The Discovery of Being*. Norton, New York.

Mayeroff, M. (1972) *On Caring*. Harper and Row, New York.

Morris, D. (1978) *Manwatching: a Field Guide to Human Behaviour*. Triad/Panther, St Albans.

Murgatroyd, S. (1986) *Counselling and Helping*. British Psychological Society/Methuen, London.

Murgatroyd, S. and Woolfe, R. (1982) *Coping With Crisis: Understanding and Helping Persons in Need*. Harper and Row, London.

Murphy, G. and Kovach, J.K. (1972) *Historical Introduction to Modern Psychology*, 6th edn. Routledge and Kegan Paul, London.

Ornstein, R.E. (1975) *The Psychology of Consciousness*. Penguin, Harmondsworth.

Pakta, F. (ed.) (1972) *Existential Thinkers and Thought*. Citadel Press, Secaucus, New Jersey.

Patton, M.Q. (1982) *Practical Evaluation*. Sage, Beverly Hills, California.

Perls, F. (1969) *Gestalt Therapy Verbatim*. Lafayette, California.

Perls, F., Hefferline, R.F. and Goodman, P. (1951) *Gestalt Therapy: Excitement and Growth in the Human Personality*. Penguin, Harmondsworth.

Pfeiffer, J.W. and Jones, J.E. (1974) (and ongoing) *A Handbook of Structured Exercises for Human Relations Training*. University Associates, La Jolla, California.

Polanyi, M. (1958) *Personal Knowledge*. University of Chicago Press, Chicago.

Pring, R. (1976) *Knowledge and Schooling*. Open Books, London.

Reibel, L. (1984) A homeopathic model of psychotherapy. *Journal of Humanistic Psychology*, **24**, 9–48.

Reich, W. (1949) *Character Analysis*. Simon and Schuster, New York.

Rogers, C.R. (1951) *Client-Centred Therapy*. Constable, London.

Rogers, C.R. (1957) The necessary and sufficient conditions of therapeutic personality change. *Journal of Consulting Psychology*, **21**, 95–104.

Rogers, C.R. (1967) *On Becoming a Person: a Therapist's View of Psychotherapy*. Constable, London.

Rogers, C.R. (1983) *Freedom to Learn for the Eighties*. Merril, Columbus, Ohio.

Rogers, C.R. (1985) Towards a more human science of the person. *Journal of Humanistic Psychology*, **25**, 7–24.

Rogers, C.R. and Dymond, R.F. (1954) (1978) *Psychotherapy and Personality Change*. University of Chicago Press, Chicago.

Rogers, C.R. and Stevens, B. (1967) *Person to Person: the Problem of Being Human*. Real People Press, Lafayette, California.

Rolf, I. (1973) *Structural Integration*. Viking Press, New York.

Ryle, G. (1949) *The Concept of Mind*. Peregrine, Harmondsworth.

Sartre, J.-P. (1956) *Being and Nothingness*. Philosophical Library, New York.

Sartre, J.-P. (1965) *Nausea*. Penguin, Harmondsworth.

Sartre, J.-P. (1973) *Existentialism and Humanism*. Methuen, London.

Schulman, E.D. (1982) *Intervention in Human Services: a Guide to Skills and Knowledge*, 3rd edn. C.V. Mosby, St Louis, Missouri.

Searle, J.R. (1983) *Intentionality: an Essay in Philosophy of Mind.* Cambridge University Press, Cambridge.

Shaffer, J.B.P. (1978) *Humanistic Psychology.* Prentice Hall, Englewood Cliffs, New Jersey.

Simon, S.B., Howe, L.W. and Kirschenbaum, H. (1978) *Values Clarification.* A and W Visual Library, New York.

Smith, E.W.L. (ed) (1975) *The Growing Edge of Gestalt Therapy.* Citadel Press, Secaucus, New Jersey.

Stewart, V. and Stewart, A. (1981) *Business Applications of Repertory Grid.* McGraw Hill, London.

Storr, A. (ed.) (1983) *Jung: Selected Writings.* Pan, London.

Tennen, H., Rohrbaugh, M., Press, S. and White, L. (1981) Reactance theory and therapeutic paradox: a compliance–defiance model. *Psychotherapy: Theory, Research and Practice,* **18**, 14–22.

Tillich, P. (1952) *The Courage to Be.* Yale University Press, New Haven, Connecticut.

Truax, C.B. and Carkuff, R.R. (1967a) *An Introduction to Counselling and Psychotherapy: Training and Practice.* Aldine, Chicago.

Truax, C.B. and Carkuff, R.R. (1967b) *Towards Effective Counselling and Psychotherapy.* Aldine, Chicago.

Vonnegut, K. (1968) *Mother Night.* Cape, London.

Wallis, R. (1984) *Elementary Forms of the New Religious Life.* Routledge and Kegan Paul, London.

Watkins, J. (1978) *The Therapeutic Self.* Human Science Press, New York.

Wheeler, D.D. and Janis, I.L. (1980) *A Practical Guide for Making Decisions.* Free Press, New York.

Wilkinson, J. and Canter, S. (1982) *Social Skills Training Manual: Assessment, Programme Design and Management of Training.* Wiley, Chichester.

Wilson, C. (1955) *The Outsider.* Gollancz, London.

Further reading

Alley, S., Blanton, J. and Feldman, R. (eds) (1979) *Paraprofessionals in Mental Health: Theory and Practice.* Human Sciences Press, New York.
Anderson, C.M. and Stewart, S. (1983) *Mastering Resistance: a Practical Guide to Family Therapy.* Guildford Press, New York.
Argyle, M. (1981) *Social Skills and Health.* Methuen, London.
Axelson, J.A. (1985) *Counseling and Development in a Multicultural Society.* Brooks/Cole, Monterey, California.
Babuscio, J. (1976) *We Speak for Ourselves: Experiences in Homosexual Counselling.* SPCK, London.
Bailey, R. (1985) *Coping with Stress in Caring.* Blackwell, Oxford.
Banville, T.G. (1978) *How to Listen – How to Be Heard.* Nelson-Hall, Chicago.
Bartlett, S.J. (1987) *When You Don't Know Where to Turn To: a Self-diagnosing Guide to Counselling and Therapy.* Contemporary Books, Chicago.
Baruth, L.G. (1987) *An Introduction to the Counselling Profession.* Prentice Hall, Englewood Cliffs, New Jersey.
Baruth, L.G. and Huber, C.H. (1985) *Counselling and Psychotherapy: Theoretical Analyses and Skills Applications.* Merrill, Columbus.
Beck, D.F. (1987) Counselor burnout in family service agencies. *Social Caseworker,* **68**, 3–15.
Belkin, G.S. (1984) *Introduction to Counseling.* Brown, Dubuque, Iowa.
Benjamin, A. (1981) *The Helping Interview,* 3rd edn. Houghton Mifflin, Boston.
Berger, D.M. (1984) On the way to emphatic understanding. *American Journal of Psychotherapy,* **38**, 111–20.
Black, K. (1983) *Short-term Counselling: a Humanistic Approach for the Helping Professions.* Addison-Wesley, London.
Blocher, D.H. (1987) *The Professional Counselor.* Macmillan, New York.
Bohart, A.C. and Todd, J. (1988) *Foundations of Clinical and Counselling Psychology.* Harper and Row, New York.
Bolger, A.W. (ed) (1982) *Counselling in Britain: a Reader.* Batsford Academic, London.
Bond, M. (1986) *Stress and Self-awareness: a Guide for Nurses.* Heinemann, London.
Bond, M. and Kilty, J. (1982) *Practical Methods of Dealing with Stress.* Human Potential Research Project, University of Surrey, Guildford, Surrey.
Brammer, L. (1973) *The Helping Relationship: Processes and Skills.* Prentice Hall, Englewood Cliffs, New Jersey.
Braswell, M. and Seay, T. (1984) *Approaches to Counselling and Psychotherapy.* Waverly, Prospect Heights, Ill.
Brown, D. and Srebalus, D.J. (1988) *An Introduction to the Counselling Process.* Prentice Hall, Philadelphia, P.A.
Brown, S.D. and Lent, R.W. (eds) (1984) *Handbook of Counselling Psychology.* Wiley, Chichester.

Burnard, P. (1987a) Counselling: basic principles in nursing. *The Professional Nurse*, **2**, 278–80.

Burnard, P. (1987b) Self- and peer assessment. *Senior Nurse*, **6**, 16–17.

Burnard, P. (1987c) Counselling skills. *Journal of District Nursing*, **6**, 157–9.

Calnan, J. (1983) *Talking with Patients*. Heinemann, London.

Campbell, A.V. (1981) *Rediscovering Pastoral Care*. Darton, Longman and Todd, London.

Campbell, A.V. (ed.) (1987) *A Dictionary of Pastoral Care*. Crossroads, New York.

Carkuff, R.R. and Pierce, R.M. (1975) *Trainer's Guide: the Art of Helping*. Human Resources Development Press, Amerhurst, Mass.

Carkuff, R.R., Pierce, R.M. and Cannon, J.R. (1977) *The Art of Helping III*. Human Resources Development Press, Amerhurst, Mass.

Cavanagh, M.E. (1982) *The Counselling Experience: Understanding and Living It*. Brooks/Cole, Monterey, California.

Chapman, E.N. and Knowdell, R.L. (1986) *Personal Counselling: a Fifty-minute Guide*. Crisp Publications, Los Altos, California.

Cheetham, J. (1977) *Unwanted Pregnancy and Counselling*. Routledge and Kegan Paul, London.

Cherniss, C. (1980) *Staff Burnout: Job Stress in the Human Services*. Sage, Beverly Hills, California.

Collins, G.R. (1988) *Innovative Approaches to Counselling*. Word Books, Waco, Texas.

Collins, M. (1983) *Communication in Health Care*. C.V. Mosby, St Louis, Missouri.

Corey, F. (1982) *I Never Knew I Had a Choice*, 2nd edn. Brooks/Cole, Monterey, California.

Corey, G. (1977) *Theory and Practice of Counselling and Psychotherapy*. Brooks/Cole, Monterey, California.

Corey, G. (1986) *Case Approach to Counselling and Psychotherapy*. Brooks/Cole, Monterey, California.

Corey, G., Corey, M.S. and Callanan, P. (1987) *Issues and Ethics in the Helping Professions*. Brooks/Cole, Pacific Grove, California.

Cormier, L.S. (1987) *The Professional Counselor: a Process Guide to Helping*. Prentice Hall, Englewood Cliffs, New Jersey.

Cormier, W.H. and Cormier, L.S. (1985) *Interviewing Strategies for Helpers: Fundamental Skills and Cognitive Behavoiural Interventions*. Brooks/Cole, Monterey, California.

Corsini, R. (1984) *Current Psychotherapies*, 3rd edn. Peacock, Itasca, Illinois.

Cox, T. (1978) *Stress*. Macmillan, London.

Dixon, D.N. and Glover, J.A. (1984) *Counselling: a Problem-solving Approach*. Wiley, Chichester.

Drum, D.J. and Knott, J.E. (1977) *Structured Groups for Facilitating Development: Acquiring Life Skills, Resolving Life Themes and Making Life Transitions*. Human Sciences Press, New York.

Dyer, W.W. and Vriend, J. (1975) *Counselling Techniques that Work: Applications to Individual and Group Counselling*. APGA Press, Washington, DC.

Edwards, P.B. (1977) *Leisure Counselling Techniques: Individual and Group Counselling Step-By-Step*, revised edn. University Publishers, Los Angeles, California.

Egan, G. (1977) *You and Me*. Brooks/Cole, Monterey, California.

Egan, G. and Cowan, R.M. (1979) *People and Systems: an Integrative Approach to Human Development*. Brooks/Cole, Belmont, California.

Ellis, A. (1973) *Humanistic Psychotherapy: the Rational Emotive Approach*. McGraw Hill, New York.

Ellis, R. and Becker, I. (1982) *A Guide to Personal Happiness*. Wiltshire, California.

Ellis, R. and Wittington, D. (1983) *A Guide to Social-skills Training*. Croom Helm, London.

Fay, A. (1978) *Making Things Better by Making Them Worse*. Hawthorne, New York.

Ferruci, P. (1982) *What We May Be*. Turnstone Press, Wellingborough.

Foggo-Pays, E. (1983) *An Introductory Guide to Counselling*. Ravenswood, Beckenham.

Gahagan, J. (1984) *Social Interaction and its Management*. Methuen, London.

Gartner, A. and Riessman, F. (1977) *Self-help in the Human Services*. Jossey Bass, San Francisco.

Gazda, G.M., Childers, D.K. and Brooks, D.K. (1987) *Foundations of Counselling and Human Services*. McGraw Hill, New York.

George, R.L. and Cristiani, T.S. (1986) *Counselling Theory and Practice*. Prentice Hall, Englewood Cliffs, New Jersey.

Gerber, S.K. (1986) *Responsive Therapy: a Systematic Approach to Counselling Skills*. Human Sciences Press, New York.

Gibson, R.L. and Mitchell, M.H. (1986) *Introduction to Counselling and Guidance*. Collier Macmillan, London.

Gilmore, S. (1973) *The Counselor in Training*. Prentice Hall, Englewood Cliffs, New Jersey.

Gladstein, G.A. and associates (1987) *Empathy and Counselling: Explorations in Theory and Research*. Springer-Verlag, New York.

Goffman, E. (1959) *The Presentation of Self in Everyday Life*. Penguin, Harmondsworth.

Goodyear, R.K. and Sinnett, E.R. (1984) Current and emerging ethical issues for counseling psychology, *Counseling Psychologist,* **12**, 87–98.

Hackney, H. and Cormier, L.S. (1979) *Counselling Strategies and Objectives*. Prentice Hall, Englewood Cliffs, New Jersey.

Hammond, D.C. and Hepworth, V.G.S. (1977) *Improving Therapeutic Communication*. Jossey Bass, San Francisco.

Hansen, J.C. (1972) *Counselling Theory and Process*. Allyn and Bacon, Boston.

Hargie, O., Saunders, C. and Dickson, D. (1987) *Social Skills in Interpersonal Communication*, 2nd edn. Croom Helm, London.

Hatcher, C., Brooks, B. and associates (1978) *Innovations in Counselling Psychology*. Jossey Bass, San Francisco, California.

Haywood, J. (1975) *Information: a Prescription Against Pain*. RCN, London.

Hendricks, G. and Weinhold, B. (1982) *Transpersonal Approaches to*

191

Counselling and Psychotherapy. Love Publishing Co, Denver, Colorado.
Herinck, R. (ed.) (1980) *The Psychotherapy Handbook*. New American Library, New York.
Heron, J. (1974) *Reciprocal Counselling Manual*. Human Potential Research Project, University of Surrey, Guildford, Surrey.
Heron, J. (1981a) *Paradigm Papers*. Human Potential Research Project, University of Surrey, Guildford, Surrey.
Heron, J. (1981b) Philosophical basis for a new paradigm, in P. Reason and J. Rowan (eds) *Human Inquiry: a Sourcebook of New Paradigm Research*. Wiley, Chichester.
Heron, J. (1982) *Education of the Affect*. Human Potential Research Project, University of Surrey, Guildford, Surrey.
Howard, G.S., Nance, D.W. and Meyers, P. (1987) *Adaptive Counselling and Therapy: a Systematic Approach to Selecting Effective Treatments*. Jossey Bass, San Francisco.
Hurding, R.F. (1985) *Roots and Shoots: a Guide to Counselling Psychotherapy*. Hodder and Stoughton, London.
Hutchins, D.E. (1986) *Helping Relationships and Strategies*. Brooks/Cole, Monterey, California.
Ivey, A.E. (1987) *Counselling and Psychotherapy: Skills, Theories and Practice*. Prentice Hall International, London.
Ivey, A.E. and Gluckstern, N.B. (1982) *Basic Attending Skills*, 2nd edn. Microtraining Associates, Amerhurst, MA.
Jacobs, M. (1985) *Swift to Hear: Facilitating Skills in Listening and Responding*. SPCK, London.
Janis, I.L. (ed.) (1982) *Counselling on Person Decisions: Theory and Research on Short-term Helping Relationships*. Yale University Press, New Haven, Connecticut.
Johnson, S.E. (1987) *After a Child Dies: Counselling Bereaved Families*. Pringer, New York.
Jung, C.G. (1976) *Modern Man in Search of a Soul*. Routledge and Kegan Paul, London.
Katz, R.L. (1971) Strategies for developing nurse empathy. *Nursing Outlook*, **19**, 714–17.
Kennedy, E. (1979) *On Becoming a Counsellor*. Gill and Macmillan, London.
Kilty, J. (1978) Self- and peer assessment. *Human Potential Research Project*. University of Surrey, Guildford, Surrey.
Kirschenbaum, H. (1979) *On Becoming Carl Rogers*. Dell, New York.
Kitchener, J.R. (1984) Intuition, critical evaluation and ethical principles: the foundation for ethical decisions in counselling psychology. *Counselling Psychologist*, **12**. 43–55.
Kottler, J.A. and Brown, R.W (1985) *Introduction to Therapeutic Counselling*. Brooks/Cole, Monterey, California.
Krumboltz, J.D. and Thorensen, C.E. (1976) *Counselling Methods*. Holt, Rinehart and Winston, New York.
Leech, K. (1986) *Spirituality and Pastoral Care*. Sheldon Press, London.
Lef'ebure, M. (ed.) (1985) *Conversation on Counselling Between a Doctor and a Priest: Dialogue and Trinity*. T. & T. Clark, Edinburgh.
Liberman, R. (1975) *Personal Effectiveness*. Research Press, Illinois.

Loughary, J.W. and Ripley, T.M. (1979) *Helping Others To Help Themselves: a Guide to Counselling Skills*. McGraw Hill, New York.

Maclean, D. and Gould, S. (1987) *The Helping Process: an Introduction*. Croom Helm, London.

Madders, J. (1980) *Stress and Relaxation*. Martin Dunitz, London.

Maple, F.F. (1985) *Dynamic Interviewing: an Introduction to Counselling*. Sage, Beverly Hills, California.

Marsella, A.J. and Pederson, P.B. (eds) (1981) *Cross-cultural Counselling and Psychotherapy*. Pergamon Press, New York.

Marshall, E.K. and Kurtz, P.D. (eds) (1982) *Interpersonal Helping Skills: a Guide to Training Methods, Programs and Resources*. Jossey Bass, San Francisco, California.

Martin, J. (1985) *Instructional Counseling: a Method for Counselors*. University of Pittsburgh Press, Pittsburgh, PA.

Maslach, C. (1981) *Burnout: the Cost of Caring*. Prentice Hall, Englewood Cliffs, New Jersey.

May, R. (1969) *Love and Will*. Norton, New York.

McIntee, J. and Firth, H. (1984) How to beat the burnout. *Health and Social Services Journal*, 9 Feb, 166–8.

Meichenbaum, D. (1983) *Coping with Stress*. Century Publishing, London.

Metge, J. and Kinloch, P. (1978) *Talking Past Each Other: Problems of Cross-cultural Communication*. Victoria University Press, Wellington, New Zealand.

Morsund, J. (1985) *The Process of Counseling and Therapy*. Prentice Hall, Englewood Cliffs, New Jersey.

Mucchilelli, R. (1983) *Face-to-face in the Counselling Relationship*. Macmillan, London.

Munro, E.A., Mantheir, R.J. and Small, J.J. (1979) *Counselling: a Skills Approach*. Methuen, Wellington, New Zealand.

Myrick, R.D. (1987) *Developmental Guidance and Counselling: a Practical Approach*. Educational Media Corp, Minneapolis.

Nelson-Jones, R. (1983) *Practical Counselling Skills: a Psychological Skills Approach for the Helping Professions and for Voluntary Counsellors*. Holt, Rinehart and Winston, London.

Nelson-Jones, R. (1984) *Personal Responsibility: Counselling and Therapy, an Integrative Approach*. Harper and Row, London.

Nelson-Jones, R. (1988) *Practical Counselling and Helping Skills: Helping Clients to Help Themselves*. Cassell, London.

Nicholson, J.A. and Golsan, G. (1983) *The Creative Counselor*. McGraw Hill, New York.

Noonan, E. (1983) *Counselling Young People*. Methuen, London.

Nurse, G. (1975) *Counselling and the Nurse: an Introduction*. HM and M, Aylesbury.

Nuttall, E.V. and Kalesnik, J. (1987) Personal violence in the schools: the role of the counselor. Special issue: Counselling and violence. *Journal of Counselling and Development*, **65**, 372–5.

O'Byrne, S. (1979) *Fundamentals of Counselling*. Frederick Press, Dublin.

Ohlsen, A.M., Horne, A.M. and Lawe, C.F. (1988) *Group Counselling*. Holt, Rinehart and Winston, New York.

Okun, B.F. (1987) *Effective Helping: Interviewing and Counseling Techniques*. Brooks/Cole, Monterey, California.

Oldfield, S. (1983) *The Counselling Relationship: a Study of the Client's Experience*. Routledge and Kegan Paul, London.

Passons, W.R. (1975) *Gestalt Approaches in Counseling*. Holt, Rinehart and Winston, New York.

Patterson, C.H. (1986) *Theories of Counselling and Psychotherapy*, 4th edn. Harper and Row, New York.

Pederson, P. (ed.) (1987) *Handbook of Cross-cultural Counselling and Therapy*. Praeger, London.

Peterson, J.V. and Nisenhoz, B. (1987) *Orientation to Counselling*. Allyn and Bacon, Newton, Mass.

Phillips, E.L. (1977) *Counselling and Psychotherapy: a Behavioural Approach*. Wiley, Chichester.

Pinkus, L. (1976) *Death in the Family: the Importance of Mourning*. Faber and Faber, London.

Priestly, P. and McGuire, J. (1983) *Learning to Help: Basic Skills Exercises*. Tavistock, London.

Procter, B. (1978) *Counselling Shop: an Introduction to the Theories and Techniques of Ten Approaches to Counselling*. Deutsch, London.

Purkey, W.W. and Schmidt, J.J. (1987) *The Inviting Relationship: an Expanded Perspective for Professional Counseling*. Prentice Hall, Englewood Cliffs, New Jersey.

Puryear, D.A. (1979) *Helping People in Crisis*. Jossey Bass, San Francisco.

Rackham, N. and Morgan, J. (1977) *Behaviour Analysis in Training*. McGraw Hill, London.

Robinson, M.D. (1988) *Meaningful Counselling: a Guide for Students, Counsellors and Clergy*. Human Sciences Press, New York.

Rogers, C.R. (1965) The therapeutic relationship: recent theory and research. *Australian Journal of Psychology,* **17**, 95–108.

Rogers, C.R. (1975) Empathy: an unappreciated way of being. *Counselling Psychologist,* **21**, 95–103.

Rogers, C.R. (1977) *On Personal Power*. Constable, London.

Rogers, C.R. (1980) *A Way of Being*. Houghton Mifflin, Boston, Mass.

Rowan, J. (1983) *The Reality Game: a Guide to Humanistic Counselling and Psychotherapy*. Routledge and Kegan Paul, London.

Rubin, S.E. and Rubin, N.M. (eds) (1988) *Contemporary Challenges to the Rehabilitation Counselling Profession*. Brookes, Baltimore.

Russell, M.L. (1986) *Behavioural Counselling in Medicine: Strategies for Modifying At-risk Behaviour*. Oxford University Press, New York.

Ryan, C.W., Jackson, B.L. and Levinson, E.M. (1986) Human relations skills training in teacher education: the link to effective practice. *Journal of Counselling and Development,* **65**, 114–16.

Sandford, C. and Beardsley, W. (1986) *Making Relationships Work*. Sheldon, London.

Sarason, S.B. (1985) *Caring and Compassion in Clinical Prctice*. Jossey-Bass, San Francisco.

Seligman, L. (1986) *Diagnosis and Treatment Planning in Counseling*. Human Sciences Press, New York.

Shertzer, B. (1980) *Fundamentals of Counselling*. Houghton Mifflin, London.

Shilling, L.E. (1984) *Perspectives on Counselling Theories*. Prentice Hall, Englewood Cliffs, New Jersey.

Sidney, E., Brown, M. and Argyle, M. (1973) *Skills with People: a Guide for Managers*. Hutchinson, London.

Skynner, R. and Cleese, J. (1983) *Families and how to Survive Them*. Methuen, London.

Smith, V.M. and Bass, T.A. (1982) *Communication for the Health Care Team*. Harper and Row, London.

Spain, J. (1987) *Sexual, Contraceptive and Pregnancy Choices: Counselling Adolescents*. Gardner Press, New York.

Stevens, J.O. (1971) *Awareness: Exploring, Experimenting, Experiencing*. Real People Press, Moab, Utah.

Stewart, W. (1979) *Health Service Counselling*. Pitman Medical, Tunbridge Wells.

Stewart, W. (1983) *Counselling in Nursing: a Problem-solving Approach*. Harper and Row, London.

Stones, G.L. (1986a) *Counseling Psychology: Perspectives and Functions*. Brooks/Cole, Monterey, California.

Stone, G.L. (1986b) Critical features and issues in research training in counselling psychology. *Counselling Psychologist*, **14**, 115–19.

Strongman, K.T. (1979) *Psychology for the Paramedical Professions*. Croom Helm, London.

Sue, D.W. (1981) *Counseling the Culturally Different*. Wiley, New York.

Talley, J.E. and Rockwell, W.J.K. (1985) *Counseling and Psychotherapy with College Students: a Guide to Treatment*. Praeger, New York.

Thompson, T.L. (1986) *Communication for Health Professionals*. Harper and Row, London.

Tilley, B.W. (1984) *Short-term Counseling: a Psychoanalytical Approach*. International Universities Press, New York.

Tipton, R.M. (1984) Trends and issues in the training and development of counseling psychologists. *Counselling Psychologist*, **12**, 111–12.

Tough, A. (1982) *Intentional Changes: a Fresh Approach to Helping People Change*. Follett, Chicago.

Tschudin, V. (1986) *Counselling Skills for Nurses*, 2nd edn. Bailiere Tindall, London.

Tyler, M. (1978) *Advisory and Counselling Services for Young People*. HMSO, London.

Van Deurzen-Smith, E. (1988) *Existential Counselling in Practice*. Sage, London.

Van Dogen, G. (1983) *Invisible Barriers: Pastoral Care and the Physically Disabled*. SPCK, London.

Venables, E. (1971) *Counselling*. The Marriage Guidance Council, London.

Vriend, J. (1985) *Counselling Powers and Passions: More Counselling Techniques that Work*. American Association for Counseling and Development, Alexandria, VA.

Wagman, M. (1984) *The Dilemma and the Computer: Theory, Research and Applications to Counselling Psychology*. Praeger, New York.

Wallace, W.A. (1986) *Theories of Counselling and Psychotherapy: a Basic-Issues Approach*. Allyn and Bacon, Boston.

Walrond-Skinner, S. (1979) *Family and Marital Psychotherapy.* Routledge and Kegan Paul, London.

Watts, A.G. (ed.) (1977) *Counselling at Work.* Papers presented by a working party of the Standing Conference for the Advancement of Counselling. Bedford Square Press, London.

Webster, E.J. (1977) *Counseling with Parents of Handicapped Children: Guidelines for Improving Communication.* Grune and Stratton, New York.

Weinstein, E. (1988) *Sexuality Counselling: Issues and Implications.* Brooks/Cole, Pacific Grove, California.

Welter, P. (1987) *Counselling and the Search for Meaning.* Word Books, Waco, Texas.

Woodcock, M. and Francis D. (1983) *The Unblocked Manager. a Practical Guide for Self-Development.* Gower, Aldershot.

Woodman, N.J. (1980) *Counseling with Gay Men and Women: a Guide for Facilitating Positive Life-styles.* Jossey-Bass, San Francisco.

Worden, J.W. (1983) *Grief Counselling and Grief Therapy.* Chapman and Hall, London.

Wright, H.N. (1986) *Self-talk, Imagery and Prayer in Counselling.* Word Books, Waco, Texas.

Wylie, T. (1980) *Counselling Young People: a Practical Introduction to Informal Counselling.* National Youth Bureau, Leicester.

Zook, A. (1987) On the merger of clinical and counselling psychology. *Professional Psychology: Research and Practice,* **18**, 4–5.

Index

AIDS Counselling 6, 122
Action following counselling 95
Advice, problems with 83
Aids to effective listening 113
Alberti, R.E. 137
Alexander, F.M. 60
Alexander technique 60
Allport, G. 37
Assumptions, counsellors 104
Attending 102, 115
Attention, zones of 102–6

Bandler, R. 53, 143
Bannister, D. 49, 50
Basic principles in counselling 66–86
Beck, A. 29
Befriending 70
Bahavioural approach in counselling 25
Behavioural aspects of listening 111
Belief systems of client and counsellor 84
Berne, E. 30, 146
Bioenergetics 60, 129
Blaming, problems in 77
Blocks in counselling, dealing with 142
Blocks to effective listening 11
Body energy, mobilisation of 136
Body, the experience of the 59
Bottling-up emotions, effects of 129–32
Bowlby, J. 95
Brandes, D. 156
Brown, R. 52
Buber, M. 70, 72, 99
Bugental, E.K. and Bugental, J.F.T. 11
Bugental, J.F.T. 12
Burnard, P. 21, 94, 156, 161

Burnout 40, 56, 132, 148–50

Campbell, A. 5, 68
Cannell, C.F. 121
Canter, S. 137, 161
Carkuff, R.R. 67
Cartesian dualism 44
Catalytic interventions 20, 167
Catharsis 131
Cathartic interventions 19, 167
Chapman, A.J. 62
Checking for understanding 124
Claxton, G. 54
Client-centred counselling 27, 70, 115–26, 171
    definition of 115
    developing skills in 178
Clift, J.C. 161
Closed questions 117
Co-counselling 150
Cognitive approach in counselling 28
Collective unconscious 45, 46
Concreteness in counselling 74–5
Confrontation in counselling 143–7
Confronting interventions 19, 167
Confronting questions 121
Congruence 53
Conscious use of self 40–2, 112, 165
Contract setting 8
Contradiction, use of in counselling 135
Corey, G. 148
Counselling
    and self-awareness 39–65
    as an act of faith 13
    basic principles 66–86
    in crisis 9
    in emotional distress 15
    as a process 2, 116

interventions 17
in spiritual distress 11
skills exercises 163–83
techniques, overuse of 85
workshops 156–62
Counter-transference 139–42
Cox, M. 89, 97, 99
Crisis
definition of 8
counselling in 9

Decision making, problems with 130
Deeper issues in counselling 89
Deluded clients 147
Depressed clients 147
Depth 99
Descartes, R. 44
Determinism 24
Dewey, J. 27
Disclosure 100
Discussion of *surface* issues 89
Disengagement from counselling 95
Dispiritedness 12, 13
Displacement of feelings 131
Don'ts in the counselling
relationship 75–8
Dreams 46
Dymond, R. 84

Eclectic approach in counselling 36
Education counselling 8
Effective counselling 22
Egan, G. 69, 74, 97, 101, 111, 161
Ellis, A. 28, 29
Embarrassment 93, 127
Emile, (Rousseau, J-J) 67
Emmons, M.L. 137
Emotional distress, counselling in 15
Emotional release 131
Emotions, types of 127–9
Empathy 69–71
Empathy building 124
Empty chair technique 134

English National Board for Nursing,
Midwifery and Health
Visiting 27
Environment for counselling 80
Epting, T.R. 33, 37, 104
Erikson, E. 12
Ernst, S. 56, 105
Evaluating learning, 161–2
Existential vacuum 12
Existentialism 82
Experiential knowledge 48, 152
Experiential learning 48, 161
Experiential learning cycle 160–1
Eye contact 111

Faith in counselling 13, 68–69
Fantasy 105
exploring 136
Fay, A. 14
Feedback from others 62
Feedback, receiving from
others 180
Feelings 55
helping with 127–138
locating in the body 134
methods of exploring 132–7
Feldenkrais, M. 60
Fiedler, F.E. 66
Finishing the counselling
relationship 95
Following in counselling 121
Fordham, F. 11
Frames of reference 83
Frankl, V.E. 12, 14
Fransella, F. 49, 50
Free association 54
exploring 173
Free-floating attention 84, 109
Freud, S. 24, 25
Funneling 121, 170

Gale, A. 62
Genuiness 72–4
definitions of 74
Gestalt approach in counselling 34

Gestalt dialogue 34, 35
Goodison, L. 56, 105
Grinder, J. 53, 143
Group exercises 174–82
Groups, learning counselling in 155

Hall, C. 24
Hallucinating clients 147
Halmos, P. 69
Harris, T. 146
Haydn, H. 39
Heron, J. 15, 17, 20, 21, 40, 47,
  52, 55, 91, 93, 112, 121, 127,
  143, 150, 156, 161, 167
Hesse, H. 13, 59
Homoepathic approach to
  counselling 13
Hopkins, G.M. 55
Humanistic approach in
  counselling 26
Humanistic psychology 27, 82
Hunches, following 58

I-it relationship 72
I-thou relationship 72, 99
Icebreakers 156
Immediacy 75
Imrie, B.W. 161
Individualion, the problems of 12
Informative counselling 6
Informative interventions 18, 167
Insight, generation of 93
Interpretation in counselling,
  problems of 83
Intuition 11, 58
Invalidating the client's feelings,
  problems in 78
Irrational beliefs 28

Jackins, H. 150
James, M. 146
Jones, J. 161
Jongeward, D. 146
Jourard, S. 100
Journal, keeping a 153

Jung, C.G. 11, 12, 45, 46, 50, 54,
  58

Kahn, R.L. 121
Kalisch, B.J. 69
Kelly, G. xi, 32, 33, 37, 54
Knowledge, types of 47
Kolb, D. 161
Kopp, S. 11
Kovach, J.K. 25

Laing, R.D. 44, 45, 50
Leaderless group activities 177, 182
Leading in counselling 121
Leading questions 120
Learning climate in counselling
  skills workshops 156–8
Learning counselling skills 85,
  152–62
  in groups 155
Levels of disclosure 89–91
Lewis, H. 162
Limitations, the counsellors 14
Limits of counselling 147
Listening to the body 60
Listening 13, 84, 102–14, 115,
  167, 169, 174
Listening, levels of 108–10
Love, moderated 68
Lowen, L. 60, 129
Luft, J. 77

Mcquarrie, J. 82
Maps of the counselling
  relationship 87–101
Marriage Guidance Council
  (RELATE) 27
May, R. 110
Mayeroff, M. 69, 72
Meaning, the search for, in
  counselling 15
Medicine 3
Meditation 60
Meeting the client 88
Mental illness 147

Minimal prompts 110
Moderated love 68
Moralising, problems in 76
Morris, D. 108
Morrison, P. 21
Murgatroyd, S. 9, 10, 115, 148
Murphy, G. 25
Mutuality 99, 100
  problems of 72
Mystifying the client 75

Needs, identifying the learning
  groups 158
Non-verbal communication 108
Noticing 40, 42–3
Nursing 3

Occupational therapy 3
Open questions 117, 118–20
Ornstein, R.E. 58
Outcomes of effective
  counselling 22
Overtalking in counselling 90
Ownership of feelings 92

Pairs, learning counselling
  in 154
Pakta, F. 82
Paradoxical interventions 13, 14
Paralinguistics 107
Parallaction 77
Patton, M.Q. 161
Peer evaluation 161, 181
Peer support 150
Perls, F. 34, 135
Perls, F., Hefferline, R.F., and
  Goodman, P. 35
Permission in counselling 80
Permission giving 132
Person, definition of 50
Personal Constructs 32
Personal Construct Approach in
  Counselling 32
Personal Construct psychology 33
Personal history, exploring 173

Personal knowledge 48
Personal qualities of the
  counsellor 67–75
Personal worlds of client and
  counsellor 83
Personhood, the concept of 49
Pfieffer, J.W. 161
Phillips, R. 156
Physiotherapy 3
Polanyi, M. 48
Portrait of the helper 69
Practical knowledge 47, 152
Prescriptive interventions 18, 167
Pring, R. 47
Problems in counselling 139–51
Problem solving 94
Programme design for counselling
  workshops 158–61
Projection 135
Prompts, minimal 110
Propositional knowledge 47, 152
Proprioception 56
Psychoanalytical psychology 43
Psychodynamic approach in
  counselling 24
Psychological approaches to
  counselling 23–38
Psychology, Schools of 1

Qualities of an effective
  counsellor 67–75
Questions, use of 117–22, 169,
  172, 175
Questions prior to counselling 79

Rational-Emotive Therapy 28
Reflection 70, 122, 170
Rehearsal 137
Reibel, L. 13
Reich, W. 60, 129
Resonance in the counselling
  process 110
Rhythm of counselling 91
Rogers, C.R. 2, 5, 12, 22, 27, 29,
  45, 48, 49, 58, 66, 67, 68, 72,

75, 84, 90, 100
Role play 154
Rolf, I. 60
Rouseseau, J-J. 27, 67
Ryle, G. 47
SOLER 111
Sanwich approach to
  confrontation 144
Sartre, J-P. 7, 13, 61, 82, 83
Schulman, E.D. 67, 72, 121
Searle, J.R. 54
Selective reflection 122, 170
Self, the 43–65
  integrated model of 50
  the inner experience of the 54
  the outer experience of the 51
Self-awareness 39–65
Self-awareness, methods of
  developing 62–5
Self-evaluation 154, 161
Self-help groups 155
Sensing 56
Separation anxiety 95
Shaffer, J.B.P. 26, 82
Shakespeare, W. 73
Shoulds and oughts, problems
  with 76, 77
Silence, coping with 142–43
Silence, exploring 179
Simon, S.B. 84
Simon, S.B., Howe, L.W. and
  Kirschenbaum, H. 13
Six category intervention
  analysis 17, 167
Skills exercises 163–83
Smith, E.W.L. 34
Social work 3
Speech therapy 3
Spiritual distress 11
Stewart, V. and Stewart, A. 33
Storr, A. 12
Streitfield, H. 161
Suicidal clients 147
Supervision 139–42
Support in counselling 139–51

Supportive counselling 4
Supportive interventions 20, 167
Surface issues, discussion of 89
Sympathy 70
Synchronicity 45

Tacit knowledge 48
Teaching 3
Telephone counselling 9
Tennen, H. 14
Therapeutic relationship, ingredients
  of 66
Thinking 54
Three stage model of counselling 97
Tillich, P. 12
Timing 79
Touch 52
Transactional analysis approach in
  counselling 30
Transference 46, 139–42
Transparency of the counsellor 100
Transpersonal domain 45
Truax, C.B. 67
Truax triad 67

Unconditional positive regard
  67–69

Value-laden questions 120
Voluntary work 3
Vonnegut, K. 137

Wallis, R. 11
Warmth, as a personal quality of the
  counsellor 72–4
Watkins, J. 110
Why questions, problems with 76,
  120
Wilkinson, J. 137, 161
Wilson, C. 13
Woolfe, R. 9
Workshops, counselling
  skills 156–62

Zones of attention 102–6